MANUEL BRITO

A Suite of Poetic Voices

Interviews with Contemporary American Poets

Kadle Books • Santa Brigida • 1992

Cover photo by Manuel Brito.

The author gratefully acknowledges the generous grant from the Spanish Ministry of
Education and Science in support of *A Suite of Poetic Voices*.

ISBN 84-88290-50-0

Contents:

FOREWORD

Undoubtedly the recent history of American poetry is characterized by the multiple and diverse energy developed by numerous poets who have definitively chosen to explore the essential matter of poetry, that is, the links between language and human beings. Actually I think we all agree that the poetic scenario in the United States can be defined as exceptional because of the richness given by the different poetics, articulating new and specific forms in approaching the poem and, especially, emphasizing a sense of exploration shared by all of them and conveying often unusual derivations from that confrontation between form and content; this is clearly visible not only among the various poetic movements but also within the evolution of individual authors. This book of interviews shows the plurality of aesthetic approaches among authors who are trying to get rid of univocality.

Nowadays the dilemma is to transform the conflicting intentions of any "odd" text into emerging hypotheses pertinent for our individual judgment, to see that any event is an invitation for the attentive reader and, of course, that each word/line/stanza/poem appears as a place for discussion. It's easy to see through those poets I've selected here that their answers and rejoinders will be variable, dissonant, concern different topics and that these creators are always interested in changing the canon. I believe, however, their ultimate ambition is to disseminate a consciousness able to reconsider the role of the individual, implying attitudes within a social or political context (Silliman and Watten). On other occasions they talk about the recovery of sensibility (Harryman), the immediacy of events such as the Gulf War (Hejinian) or merely show the fragmentation and reconciliation of our reality (Armantrout and Scalapino).

The interviews or questionnaires emerged as a concrete way of exhibiting the characteristics of those poetries and poetics of this complex age. Usually all the questions try to motivate rather than to assert categorically about his/her way of writing. In this sense, all of them have shown their "different narrative" reaching the bottom of their thoughts, tracking the traces of their identities. They speak about their ability to mould a new poetic paradigm and, of course, they pay attention to their craft and formal derivations. As key figures of this second half of the twentieth century they recognize that there's a common argument: language as the primary matter that reflects the inner nature of human beings. The modernist authorial artist has given way to a generator poet from whom we acknowledge multiple subjectivities.

The only admissible coherence is to trascend conventionality and this can be carried out in opposition to a facile reading, distorting the aesthetic value of cultural forms, tracing new ideological implications... Even more, repetitions acquire new substance, denials will turn into approvals, there will be vague recognitions and significant mistakes can be clarified intuitively. Anyway, we are immersed in this contemporary context and they are re-viewing its true nature.

I am sure those readers who approach these interviews will read and interpret beyond the literalness of the answers and intentions of these poets, exploring and dis-covering a true, open, and sometimes ambivalent poetry that characterizes their own literary production. There are also some very recent poetic movements who have reacted against this sort of poetry, speaking about the crisis and exhaustion of new formulations to be assimilated by the general public. Perhaps we have to notice that diversity and controversial oppositions have taken the place of those established cultural manifestations that avant-garde movements always struggled against. The poets who appear in this book don't represent the enormous variety of the actual American poetic scenario but they come to show us a new strategy to perceive the transformation of art before experience and reality.

Acknowledgements

I feel a special debt to Michael Davidson who invited me to the University of California at San Diego and who has persevered in his encouragement. Also special thanks to Jerome Rothenberg who has helped me so much in understanding poetry. I am thankful for assistance to staff members of the Archive for New Poetry at UCSD. I wish to express my gratitude to Antonio and Carlos Suárez for the production of this book.
And definitely to all of the poets included in this book.

RAE ARMANTROUT

Photo by Manuel Brito

Rae Armantrout's case is particularly fascinating for me since her poetry seems to be apparently dislocated, character-ized by a deindividualized substance. In spite of this I think she plays intuitively with her own ontologization and the ultimate projection on the reader. Though the text appears as the leit motif of her poetry, I suspect that her final narrative intention is to picture her life and society through dispersed images. That's why the tension between the individual and the crowd deserves immediate recognitions for we assume that the event/ text will be continually reinterpreted. Even in this questionnaire she does not answer categorically but prefers to show herself as a bricoleur with the confidence that she has to take risks in order to gain visibility and honesty in her approach to the text itself. Born in Vallejo (CA) in 1947 she graduated from San Francisco State University. Among her books of poetry we have **Extremities** (1978), **The Invention of Hunger** (1979), **Precedence** (1985), and **Necromance** (1991).

Q: How would you describe your method of writing which is determined by that multiple edgeness that sends us to different centers of perception?

A: You seem to be asking about the role of disjunction (and coherence) in my poems. It's true that they seldom manifest a single image, scenario or procedure. What I am most interested in are complex, oblique relations between stanzas or sections. Typically one of my poems would deal with an abstract *subject* in a series of discrete and concrete ways. An example might be the second section of the poem "Character Development" from my new book **Necromance**.

> This is the cry
> that Mother recognized!
>
> So Maxim Lord has faked his death.
> The plot was hatched by Captain Britain
> to protect his Son,
> recuperating in MurderWorld.

These two stanzas are very different in tone and in the type of discourse they suggest. One can't imagine the same voice speaking them. The first is intimate and experiential while the second is a quote from a comic book. On the other hand, both stanzas deal with some sort of parental care and both refer (in different ways) to the title concept –character development. Their juxtaposition *appears logical*– if the child can still cry then he must not be dead –but since these are different types of characters, the second actually undercuts the first. The parts are working against as well as with one another. Perhaps this is the *multiple edgeness* to which you refer.

Q: I've observed that in your poetry there are encounters and misencounters, an entrance into the private that is dissolved into the materiality of words and incomplete units, is there an intent of writing self-mirroring poems?

A: Well, my poems are composed, to a great extent, of what I happen to see and hear –and then, immediately, what those sights and sounds cause me to think about. So my personal (home and neighborhood) experience is very much part of the poems. Does that mean they are *self-mirroring* or autobiographical? That depends on how we define the self –which is a question which usually interests me. I'm interested in the conjunction of self and culture. Are our thoughts our own? We are discrete genetic entities and yet each of us had her first words put in her mouth by her parents and grew up to join the pre-existing discourse of her time. The first stanza of my poem "Attention" (from **Necromance**) is

> Ventriloquy
> is the mother tongue.

That may be a provocative over-statement, but it identifies a concern I have.

A newer poem, "Confidential" reads in part,

> On the inscribed surface
> of sleep:

> Almost constant
> bird soundings.

> "Aloha, Fruity Pebbles!"
> ...

Many Americans would know that Fruity Pebbles is a breakfast cereal advertised on television. Here even the seemingly private element of sleep is inscribed by social text. I heard this commercial as I was drowsing. It's impossible to say whether the poem mirrors my life or the life of our age.

Q: Usually the addressee in your poems is a *you* who is verbalized ghostly since there's little context for his/her formalization, in this sense you seem to follow Sapir when he says '*ideation reigns in supreme language...*'

A: The pronouns are fairly arbitrary in my poetry. I would imagine this is so for many other writers as well. Like the characters in dreams, pronouns are aspects of oneself. I may choose a pronoun for the tone it creates. For instance, using *you* can make a poem sound either seductive or confrontational. I provide *little* context for these pronouns partly because I am not necessarily trying to establish them as solid identities, separate from myself. I'm interested in the multiplicity, and also the duplicity, of inner voices. I am not quite sure how your quote from Sapir follow from your observation on my work, however, the ideation is the process of forming ideas –that is more than one. Thinking may be mainly sensing relations. I can connect ideation in this way with my interest in internal voices.

Q: You seem very conscious on non interpreting but of suggesting reflections through questions, open sentences, etc. But also it seems to be an instinctive discourse looking for the pleasure of now and some emotional impasses...

A: I want poetry to have the speed and urgency of thought. I could say that I am neither *interpreting* nor *suggesting reflections* –rather I am, in fact, reflecting. But that ignores the problem of audience. Poetry involves displaying one's mental processes first to oneself and then to others. In the context of display, sincerity is problematic, yet I would agree with Oppen that, however elusive, sincerity is the measure and goal of the poem. That may sound strange coming from someone who has written '*Ventriloquy/ is the mother tongue.*' That line shows the extent of my pessimism. I don't believe we'll ever arrive at truth or sincerity, but I think we'd better keep trying. There *is* a pleasure in encountering an impasse (emotional or otherwise). It is paradoxically, an indication that we are on the way. This is beginning to sound like **Pilgrim's Progress**. Speaking of ventriloquy, this must be the voice of my protestant upbringing. I think people often impose unity on a poem (or a nation for that matter) in order to look good before some imagined audience. I try to avoid that.

Q: I think you try to transcend the polemics about writing like a woman or concerning exclusively to archetypal functions, is there recognitions of a more communal experience?

A: I think a close reading of my work reveals that it is the product of a woman's life. Still, when I was in my twenties, I was actually told by two separate men that I *"wrote like a man."* All they meant, I suspect, is that I didn't write as exclusively about romantic difficulties as they imagined a woman would or should. Such prescriptions seem arbitrary. These days there is a more sophisticated attempt to define the feminine. Feminist theories have said that a female writing, for instance, might have a kind of limitless sensuousity. It would eschew logic and have no real beginning or end. That's an attractive idea, but I still distrust definitions. At any rate, the writing they describe is not exactly like my own. I am compelled by starts and stops, silences, and (the trappings of) logic. I often use logic comedically, but I am perversely fascinated by it. I don't think it will be easily jettisoned. I find that, however it's framed, I resist the systematization of masculinity and femininity. Paradoxically, I feel most female when I am resisting or subverting systems.

Q: One of the most consistent commentaries about your poetry comes from Ron Silliman who emphasizes your sensibility in exploring unnoticed facets of the verbal art, is there a special grammar for inventing those mysteries without boundaries?

A: I always thought Silliman was talking about exploring unnoticed facets of social reality in general, not only the *verbal art*. Certainly his own writing renders the sights, sounds and smells of a neighborhood as well as the vicissitudes of the writing process. That's something I very much admire in Ron's work. Likewise, when I want to write poetry (as opposed to some other kind of writing) the first thing I do is *"stop, look,* *and listen"* as the kindergartners are instructed to do before they cross a street.

I would like a grammar to produce *"mysteries without boundaries."* I'm attracted by things I don't understand and often write about them. I like ending a poem with a statement which is satisfactory at first, but troubling on second thought. At that point, one has to go back —but how far?

CHARLES BERNSTEIN

Photo by Susan Bee

This restless writer who is continually renewing the poetic form informs us about poetry as composition, considering it as an orchestration of different elements (sound, line, word, punctuation, etc.) and showing a particular interest in experimenting and permitting the mind of the reader to fix a variety of concepts. His exploratory sense in poetry allows him to re-evaluate the material signs of reality and their connection with language. Born in New York in 1950, he attended Harvard University. His bibliography shows the creative fertility of this poet who works as David Gray Professor of Poetry and Letters at the State University of New York at Buffalo. Among others he has published such books as **Asylum** (n.d.), **Parsing** (1976), **Shade** (1978), **Poetic Justice** (1979), **Senses of Responsibilities** (1979), **Controlling Interests** (1980), **Disfrutes** (1981), **The Occurrence of Tune** (1981), **Stigma** (1981), **Islets/Irritations** (1983), **Resistance** (1983), **The Sophist** (1987), **Veil** (1987), **Four Poems** (1988), **The Nude Formalism** (1989), **The Absent Father in Dumbo** (1990), **Rough Trades** (1991), **Fool's Gold** (1991). He also collaborated in **Legend** (1980) and his most important book of essays is **Content's Dream: Essays 1975-1984**. His role as an editor of **L=a=n=g=u=a=g=e** (1978-1981), **The L=a=n=g=u=a=g=e Book** (1984) and **The Politics of Poetic Form** (1990) has also exerted a determinating influence in the American poetic scene.

Q: Could you be defined as a "demanding poet" looking for answers?

A: I'm more looking for questions, constantly trying to upturn any set way of putting things, although, in the process, I do hover in proximity to something like answers, if responding, or being answerable to yourself, to your language, is an answer. I suppose I make a lot of presumptions in my work, in that the poems don't explain themselves. What interests me in a phrase or line is not always self-evident, it's only that it strikes me. I demand a lot from the materials (the words and the connections among them), but then, it seems like they demand a lot from me. Yet I'm never far from what's for me, anyhow, verbal pleasure, because if you demand a lot from words all of sudden they start to talk back to you in the most intimate and also engaging way, and that engagement has a lot to do with the intensified soundscape of the poem and also with the acceleration of play (puns, rimes, misnomers, vowel and consonant repetition, and the dozens of other related devices of a trade in language). I figure if a reader or listener can't make out a particular reference or train of thought, that's okay –it's very much the way I experience things in everyday life. If the poem is at times puzzling or open-ended or merely suggestive, rather than explicit, maybe it gives readers or listeners more space for their own interpretations and imaginations. Different readers pick up different things and for any reader certain allusions are bound to be striking while others will seem opaque, but which is which changes from reader to reader. What I like in poems is encountering the unexpected and I enjoy not knowing where I am or what comes next.

Which means I try to derail trains of thoughts as much as follow them; what you get is a mix of different types of language pieced together as in a mosaic –very "poetic" diction next to something that sounds overheard, intimate address next to philosophical imperatives, plus a mix of would-be proverbs, slogans, jingles, nursery rhymes, songs. I love to transform idioms as much as traditional metrics because I'm looking to say things I can only say in poems; I'm, driven by that necessity. Sometimes there's a gap between sentences, sometimes the sound or sentiment carries over that gap: these shifting, modulated transitions express my philosophy as much as my prosody.

For me poetry and poetics are not so much a matter of how I can make words mean something I want to say but rather letting language find ways of meaning through me. Form is never more than an extension of sound and syntax: the music of poetry is the sound of sense coming to be in the world. –I wouldn't know an answer if it stood on my head. A good joke, though... that's a different matter.

Q: You affirm in "Amblyopia" (in *The Sophist*)that we have to assume the spirit of balance, in which sense?

A: That's the section about the "rate on purchase" and "the balance of every purchase". I loved the strains of Puritan sermon that run through this passage, lifted verbatim from the back of a credit card bill, and set in lines. One of the many "fine print" language types that are constantly at the periphery of consciousness, but which we rarely focus on. I only focussed on it myself because I was reading it aloud as part of a proofreading job. Is this the poetry of everyday life, a discrete particular? –well, only in my twisted (twisting) sense of these things. Or do things like our credit card contracts provide an allegory for a spiritual or religious contract we've entered into –as if, in a consume-on-credit society we are, indeed, each judged by the balance of (and on) our purchases, and where our purchase is much more than a dinner or a couch, but a "purchase" in the figurative sense of that word, a position of advantage in the world, for which we may not be prepared to pay the bill, unaware of the hidden charges.

I've never been much for balance, but there's clear advantage to staying on your feet or not falling off the bed. I was a slow learner (which I suppose may be why I like to teach): it found it difficult to reproduce socially prized models of balance, symmetry and grace; no doubt I grew to resent these things, more often conventions than the immutable principals they purported to be. It seemed to me I kept my balance in some mighty awkward ways: it may be my aesthetic now, but it was largely given to me by disadvantage. Disadvantage, that is, puts you in mind of your particular vantage and that enables some sort where posture, say, or grammar, is not the only factor. Within a poem, the more active questions of eco-balance are one of proportion and judgment. I think what may make my work seem difficult is that I am always testing my judgments, throwing them this interrogation, of judgment and senses of proportion constitute the aesthetic process for me.

On balance, I am reminded of a remark made by Wittgenstein to his sister, Hermine: "You remind me of somebody who is looking out through a closed window and cannot explain to himself the strange movements of a passerby. He cannot tell what sort of storm is raging out there or that this person might only be managing with difficulty to stay on his feet." When the reader is sealed off from the world of the poem, it may well seem strange and demanding; it is only when you get a sense for this world, and not just the words, that the poem can begin to make sense.

Q: Sometimes you seem to be really concerned about the arrangement of lines, a preoccupation you share with poets such as Pound or Olson. How does this aspect affect your mode of writing?

A: Preoccupation is a good way to put, ever so much nicer than obsession, which is one way to look a recurring interest that has no rhyme or reason. I'm attracted to the idea of lines being a primarily visual feature of the poem –it's a modest way of designing (or arranging) how the page looks, an overlay –one more dynamic of the poems multi-layered ecosystem.

Often I don't leave pauses for the line breaks when I perform a poem, which suggests that they are not principally related to the temporal soundtext (or phonotext). But then again, in performance, there are many more ways to cue different tones, voices, rhythms, beats, and phrasing than on the page, that the line becomes a crucial device for setting such things in motion. If the line is relatively independent of the phonotext, then that's one of its great advantages, because you can play with the peculiarly visual space of the page, which is a particular feature of writing as opposed to spoken language or other nonverbal signifying practices. Given my interest in interruption (more than fragmentation), the line allows for a visual interruption of the phrase (or sentence) without necessarily requiring a temporal interruption, a pause: that's why I so often cut the line where you are least likely to pause (say between and article and a noun). When you break the line against the phrase, rather than at the end of a phrase, it's called syntactic scissoring; this preoccupies me because I can use it to set in motion a counter-measure that adds to the rhythmic richness of the poem: the main measure in the phrasally forward movement of the phonotext, and the countermeasure of the syntactic scissoring of the visual text.

I'm mindful of Dennis Tedlock's useful discussion of the line as a device for registering oral dynamics of native American verbal art. Tedlock's use of the line in his translations/transcriptions is as far from traditional prosody as anything any else modernist poetry has come up with. Tedlock roundly condemns the use of prose to convey the hyperdynamic soundscape of oral literature, and has developed ways to cue not just different lengths of pausing, but also pitch, loudness, and other features of the phonotext. I'm very attracted to the acoustic tactility both of the oral literature he is attending to and also his ways of transforming it into a multitextured writing. ("Writing wrongs speech," as Neil Schmitz puts it in his book on Twain and Stein.)

In creating an aural poetry, I think it's possible to have the resonant presence of language without hypostatizing a single speaker as the source of the language. Writing, that is, can become answerable to itself in ways that do not advance upon orality but are co-present with it. To do this, however, writing cannot revert to the conditions of orality, nostalgically imagining itself as secondary, as transcript of the voice, but rather must acknowledge its own materiality and acoustic density/destiny, its visible aurality.

Q: *Poetic Justice* and *Disfrutes* are characterized by the objectual dimension of the word itself, you play with the typography, sound and a certain disorientation at the level of content. Would you explain more profoundly the purposes of your position?

A: Disfrutes, my earliest published work, basically plays on slight shifts in sound patterns and miniature word arrangements. The most minimal is four one-word lines" "sand/ and/ sane/ an" which follows the *an* sound through to itself. I still find this kind of progression curiously satisfying, even though I wouldn't isolate it the way I did in **Disfrutes**: but it does typify the kind of detail I use in composing my by now rococo works. In **Poetic Justice** I intErrUPT woRds by uSiNg caPitAL lETTeRs tO cREaTe A kiNd of pulsInG eNergY: again with the idea that interruption and disruption actually create intensity and rhythm, by emphasizing the physical qualities both of the sound and the visual representation of words.

Q: Can the films you realized with Henry Hills be seen under this same perspective?

A: What Henry's done is to create a phonotext, a.k.a. soundtrack, by splicing together small bits of sync-sound film, often just a few seconds each. It's an incredible mosaic, which exemplifies the sort of constructed aurality I've been discussing.
One way I write poems is to assemble, create an order for, an increasingly wild variety of bits, units, bytes, hits, sections, units, phrases –segments. Hills shoots in sync sound then cuts the shoots into short 'scenes'. The soundtrack is made by physically splicing these scenes –bits of sync sound/image– together. Focussing just on the acoustic level, he is creating, by

this process, a sound poem, or collage text.

Still, there are crucial differences between film and poetry. One of the main differences, retrievability, the ability to reread, review, specified moments, is beginning to vanish. When Hills's films are seen in video, you'll be able to slow them up, stop them, a viewing situation that approaches, without ever intersecting, reading a book. In contrast, a screening of the film would more closely parallel hearing a poet perform a work. Two different performance modes are now available.

There's another aspect, however. Because it's in sync sound, meaning that all the sound was recorded live, whenever the sound is cut-up you also have the *picture*, and therefore a gesture, also cut-up. Accompanying the sound is always this outward picture *–a body*. When Henry's editing the particular sound or syllable or phrase –sequencing segments– you have in each segment, in addition to the sound, the movement, the gestures of the body. That's again the extraordinary thing about the films, that the sound is simultaneously registered as gestures of the body, the sound embodies even as it is cut-up, dislocated from its original context. In Hills's films, there is an elaborate scoring or choreography of these gestures.

Q: Is experimentation, as an active process, sufficient by itself?

A: That would be true for some of the works of Jackson Mac Low or John Cage or William Burroughs –works that are a valuable resource for my writing. My own preoccupations, however, are not with experimentation as much as evocation, instantiation, arbitration, and reclamation.

Q: The quotidian, or elements related to our daily life are present in many of your poems. What is your interest in this approach?

A: Another preoccupation: the ordinary, a tradition more often associated with a plainer style than mine, but then what could be more everyday than words? It's a strange pull, since even then I often use arcane, rather than everyday, words. But it's the texture of everyday experience I'm after, how language both contains and engenders experience. And many of the particulars that litter my poems are indeed everyday sayings (sometimes inverted) and overhead comments. Moreover, the mix of elements, including the discontinuity and interruption, is part of the fabric of everyday life in the present.

Q: *Veil* is introduced by a quotation from Hawthorne's *The Minister's Black Veil*. How can be understood the metaphor of the veil as applied to your poetry?

A: Let me finish up by answering that question together with your next one, about the " 'us'ness" I write about in **Content's Dream**?

Veil is my most visually oriented work. The visual emblem is produced by several layers of overtyping, so that much, but not all, of the freely composed writing is obliterated. One model I had was Morris Louis's "Veil" paintings, where successive stains of colors occlude the inner layers, though at the edges the brightest of the suppressed underlayers of color, shines through, ecstatically.

The sense of stain, as in soiling, and its associated sadness, is crucial; but also, as in biochemistry, the stain allowing you to identify otherwise invisible substances. In this sense, my poetry

is an acoustic staining. That's why I'm inclined to dwell on (in)
forms of damage, maladjustment, dislocation. This is not an
aesthetic theory so much as an experiential dynamic –call it the
everyday: that we have our misalignments more in common
than our adjustment to the socially correct norms. Normalcy is
the enemy of poetry –my poetry, "our" poetry.
When today's **New York Times** (8/19/92) runs a piece on out-
of-sync" kids and how "we" can help them fit in, I see my
poetics (and their debt to Hawthorne, Thoreau, and Emerson)
spelled out in reverse. "We've all known children like this,"
Jane Brody begins, "they stand too close or they touch us in
annoying ways; they laugh too loud or at the wrong times; they
make "stupid" or embarrassing remarks,... they mistake friendly
actions for hostile ones,... they move too slowly, or too fast, for
everyone else; their facial expressions don't jibe with what
they or others are saying, or their experience is seriously out
of step with current fashions." While I both identify and try to
attend to such differences, peculiarities and idiosyncracies of
perception, the article predictably prescribes the psychological
orthodontics of correction and behavioral modification to
obliterate the dis-ease, which is given the high-fallutin' name
of dyssemia (flawed signal reception), a suitable companion
discipline to my own poetic preoccupation, dysraphism.
The veil acknowledges the stigma that is our common ground,
our point of adjacency with one another, our 'us"ness. Here,
Veil is related to a short book of my poems called **Stigma**,
based on the title of one of Erving Goffman resonant books on
this topic.
In the Hawthorne story, the minister who veils his face gives
an explanation that I use as the epigraph for the book: "There
is an hour to come when all of us shall cast aside our veils.
Take it not amiss, beloved friend, if I wear this piece of crape

till then." Our bodies veil is from transparency (say, assimilation) and the veil acknowledges that: that we can't communicate as if we had no veils or bodies or histories separating us, that whatever communication we can manage must be in terms of our opacities and particularities, our resistances and impermeabilities –call it our mutual translucency to each other. Our language is our veil, but one that too often is made invisible. Yet, hiding the veil of language, its wordness, its textures, its obstinate physicality, only makes matters worse. Perhaps such veils will be cast aside in the Messianic moment, that utopian point in which history vanishes. On this side of the veil, which is our life on earth, we live within and among the particulars of a here (hear) and now (words that speak of and to our condition of everydayness).

NORMA COLE

Photo by Michael Lebowitz

Norma Cole answered my questionnaire on her poetry and poetics with a series of poems. By so doing she returned me to more questionings and endless explorations. Undoubtedly this form of cognition becomes the most tautological speech of the whole book. The questions I asked her were suggested so that she explain her poetic method characterized by the lack of punctuation, a distinctive syntax which is mostly carried by the nouns and adjectives, also about her progression from basic reality to a more abstract sense of it, the role of painting in her poems and what conveys for her a line such as "silence notes its own misreadings." This heterological poetry generates various perceptions through fragmentation. Sequencing of lines, repetitions of certain devices, and recognition make us continually rethink the certainty of their relation to the context. Notice again that her task produces meanings, concepts, and games with the syntax used in those poems but, in fact, we know she informs us about Western culture in order to argue about ourselves. She was born in Canada and she has written among other books **Mace Hill Remap** (1988) and **Metamorphosia** (1988).

Dear Manuel Brito,

Nothing equals the "There is".* There is no match for it. One response is to write. Since it is impossible for me to give 'straight answers' to your thought-out questions, my response is this brief introductory note along with "What Others Had Told Me", my most recent writing. The occasion for this piece was a benefit, a gathering, really, of the community of writing in the Bay Area that is currently being presented in O Press books and anthologies. These group readings are fascinating in that they focus attention on the extent to which writing is produced "in community", as a function of individuals' engagement with issues of concern to others –or not. The continuum represents itself. It evidences the freedom to do so. "One only writes through love..."** An American poet once said to me, "People write from their eros, but you, you write from your phobos." I would say "both", and I would say that what I think to ask writing is continuously addressed in everything I write.

Sincerely,

Norma Cole

* Emmanuel Levinas, "There Is: Existence without Existents."
** Deleuze & Parnet, *Dialogues.*

What Others Had Told Me

On the anniversary of Fact we had marched into bed with them
and paid with extraordinary rage

A grazing field masking the toxic canal, capped and causal,
removing the deaf signs

How they treated objects without arms, an admirable ideal

Where to place the stops grew out of a sensible idea, a sequence
of notes

Incomplete knots that snow that critique of nuts was a dead end

Refer me to the nearest altar, layered, all remote

Psychoanalysis is a piece of cake, a kind of medieval positivism
I can't put my finger on, being reducible to attraction repulsion

We have imported our jobs

News just keeps on coming

What is questionable in the production of a text, its evidence
and the history of all experience

Theirs or in turning one's back going through it heuristically,
choosing the specificity

Searching for a language where the u comes before the q

The piano disappeared or there had never been a glad hand
equal to your structure

At first it seemed additive then holds back, not necessarily
narrative but told

Puffy clouds once considered the representation of a cultivated
field have been a representation ever since

Have ever seen its shine

Since at first here is the custom to make bread in the shape of
dolls, died purple with berries

One must become more self-reliant, more nineteenth-century,
a globe of empiricism

Scarcely waking to this "plaster" in this the last moment of life

Wouldn't eat the least of the burnt part

Sticks and strawberry jam under plastic on the mountain

Think and need
tooth and nail
and on either side of the peak an ear

Old wares or the town of Once Was, dust balls, feathers, "hatred emplacements"

Throw a button in the air

Or go on trips with reading privileges "I did"

From the free world you could hear laughing, children with teeth missing visiting the voices earned out of gravity

From the Plain of the Liberation the Blood Bath Party, a family fund, the corners not touching

Any corners

Suddenly a doorway white like a cake croaking there are no sides

The only stranger was authenticity, tepid content, food, money, versification

Medicine bundles and what others had told me

Small ones in their hair

It was only tactical that unnerved him but his interests were too scattered and unprofessional to go through with this sky so clearly

For years this brandishing their chops before the flies settle

Who hesitates to throw a manual practical control never filled,
attractively served

The pop slap I heard
I *personally* had seen
the treatment unit
the cells

Book, think of something, astral projection stuck to the wall

The name is arcing across, making distinctions with unholy
certainty

Barely given
and then its anagram

Overrun house and cuts in return for blood

With the intention of summarizing and ends determine the
unfolding to acknowledge, to credit, to be explicit

Patient body more reasonable, more unrecognizable–
–possibility is not knowledge

Facts loom up like icebergs at 37,000 feet

Leaving order as a way of starting over it's impossible to
repeat

MICHAEL DAVIDSON

Photo by Manuel Brito

Michael Davidson asserts that his poetic craftsmanship came from the book, **Understanding Poetry**, by Cleanth Brooks and Robert Penn Warren along with those stern lectures he attended at Creative Writing workshops that became an "inhospitable atmosphere" for him. However they all helped him to write a poetry that became interested in the explanation of its own processes and definitively "to test the thresholds of meaning." I think that, in fact, Davidson's academic achievement causes him to be perceived as a poet who manages to use skillfully the different mechanisms for building and representing the links of our quotidian activities along with theoretical reflection about literature. He is immersed in searching for and reconciling the absolute and the fragile, banality and certainty, but always inscribed within harmonic lines. Born in Oakland and graduated from the State University of New York, Buffalo, he is Professor of Literature at the University of California, San Diego. His main books of poetry are **Exchanges** (1972), **Two Views of Pears** (1973), **The Mutabilities and the Foul Papers** (1976), **Summer Letters** (1976), **Grillwork** (1980), **Discovering Motion** (1980), **The Prose of Fact** (1981), **The Landing of Rochambeau** (1985), **Analogy of the Ion** (1988), **Post Hoc** (1990). He has also been the editor of **The Archive Newsletter** and **Documents for New Poetry**; his essays on the San Francisco Renaissance and American poetry have helped to clarify decisively the recent and contemporary literary scene.

Q: Your poetry is characterized by the presence of emotional motives along with metalinguistic devices and referential elements. How should this macrocomplex structure be defined?

A: The two are synonymous. "Emotional motives" and "metalinguistic devices" are not the ends and means of poetry but two ways of identifying the same thing. I often begin writing because I feel a certain way about something, but once the words appear they restructure how that emotion is experienced. Writing becomes a constant exchange of claims and counter-claims by one's inherited language *not* to be adequate to an experience that seems to lie beyond it. If language were adequate to either "emotional motives" or "referential elements," we would stop writing altogether. Use of the "metalinguistic" signals that one is alive to that fact.

Q: You are one of the few younger poets who includes a lot of references to traditional mythology along with proper names of friends. Can this be seen as an archaeology of re-acknowledgements and re-discoveries in the Duncanian sense?

A: What you describe as "Duncanian" is a modernist need to write oneself into "the tradition," however heretical that tradition may be. The use of mythological or personal names among my contemporaries is often an attempt to invoke a realm of narrative or person with all of the associations "Hermes" or "Plato" might imply. On the one hand, such usage is a recognition that people have names and that the poem is a place where they can be spoken to (whether they are fictional nor not); on the other, when I speak of the Minotaur in the opening poem of **Prose of Fact**, I'm conscious of the maze, Theseus' thread and so forth –narrative elements that help develop a reflection on time and presence. When I speak of Max Weber in "Mixed Aryan" **(Post Hoc)**, I'm not so much interested in his sociological theories as I am in his name as a marker of some kind of ultimate theorizing about society (and which contrasts with the genealogical theme of the poem). For the modernist, names are sites of cultural development and authority; for a younger generation (which certainly learned from poets like Duncan) names become markers for unpronounceable areas of one's experience.

Q: Mukarovsky said that the theoretical function of language is one of the sources of new metaphors and metonymies. Paradoxically it seems to me that contemporary American poets (especially the so-called language poets) provoke multiple and interchangeable situations and meanings, but at the same time they compel us to primary and simple concepts...

A: If I understand you correctly, you're saying that there is a contradiction between Mukarovsky's theory of foregrounding (that poetic language exploits its rhetoricity) and contemporary poetry's skepticism about figuration, its preference for flat, uninflected language. I suppose that if you were to take the specific examples used by members of the Prague school (or

Moscow or Leningrad circles) and compare it, say, to the poetry of Silliman or Watten, there would be a contradiction since the latter tend to draw very much on the *doxa*, the speech acts of daily parlance. But the primary emphasis of Mukarovsky's theory involves a general tendency within poetry to reject instrumentality, the "predatory intent," as Zukofsky called it, of language in service to its consumers. In this respect, the various Slavic schools of poetics have much in common with contemporary counter-poetics in the U.S. Where language-writing departs from Mukarovsky is its belief that literary foregrounding involves an ideological and political intervention into *doxa*, not just an aesthetic deformation of it.

Q: Is it true that we are living by metaphors as George Lakoff suggests in his book?

A: Yes and no.

Q: In some of your books, especially in *The Landing of Rochambeau* and *Post Hoc* there are not only unfoldings of meaning in time but also in space (poems such as "Rewrite", etc.). How would you analyze this process?

A: Jakobson speaks of the poetic function as projecting the "principle of equivalence from the axis of selection into the axis of combination" which to me means that words in poetry cease to be sequences and become figures. It means that everything is recombined, no matter how much the author strives for verisimilitude. I'm interested in history in the books you name, but I'm also interested in history as written, as figured, as figural. When I wrote "The Landing of Rochambeau," I was fascinated with a story of which I knew absolutely nothing and yet which was very much a part of my cultural background. By juxtaposing the event (the landing of Rochambeau) with my act of writing about it, I was able to understand something fundamental about history: that it never "unfolds in time" but is experienced piecemeal, fragmentarily. It is only in the hands of those who seek to use events for coercive purposes, that history appears to be linear. How, then, to de-fuse that tendency?

Q: In many of your poetic prose pieces I've observed a mixture of flashes/statements along with an evident irony which transcends the discourse implicit in it. Is it a matter of encoding and decoding thoughts?

A: I wish it were as complex as that. My use of irony doesn't have much of the sense of "control" attached to it that we associate with Eliot or the New Critics. I use irony in the same way that I use flat, declarative diction –to register the specific context of an utterance. That is, I don't think there is a "neutral" diction for which poetry is the aberration (and for which irony is the master trope). Rather, I think we speak in public spaces to actual human beings (even when we are talking to "ourselves"), and we alter the register of our speech to accommodate a specific speech act situation. Rather than transcending discourse, irony is one form that talk takes.

Q: I think that the narrator of your prose poems is very strong individually and very singular. I mean, it's difficult to perceive his voice as belonging to "an autre." Is he the target of his own rhetoric?

A: I certainly hope so. As I said above, names –and in this case, pronouns– are markers or positions that can be manipulated to signify different levels of identity. I'm surprised that you find the narrator of my prose to be so singular since I try to refract singularity into a number of "persons." But perhaps this is, in itself, a sign of the unitary subject –the inability of the writer to escape some kind of egocentric sense of self. And as much as I would like to feel that I am being spoken through, in Spicer's sense of reception, it's always my voice through which the "other" comes. But even Spicer was aware that if you want to speak in the tongues of men and angels but have a cleft palette, you will speak with a cleft palette.

Q: I've observed that in some of your essays there is an interest in the political substructure of language, that is, an interest in the different meanings as derived from language in connection with social facts. Would you say that it is impossible for there to be a pure and exact communicational function in our contemporary age?

A: Yes, but I don't think there ever was a "pure and exact communicational function" in any age. What characterizes the period since the evolution of philological and linguistic sciences in the nineteenth-century has been an increasing consciousness about the mediated nature of language. At first it was necessary to describe the historical evolution of root-systems, but with figures as different as Volosinov or Sapir or Benveniste, it became necessary to speak of the "productive" nature of linguistic structures. That is, not only was it necessary to talk about the historical evolution of language, it was also necessary to describe its role in structuring history itself. Thus what looked like the base or "substructure" turns out to have an ideological componant insofar as meanings become sedimented in usage. Poetry, to adopt a phrase of Luce Irigaray's, "jams the technology," by which ideology does its work, but poetry does this in noninstrumental ways. By treating language as a system, it attacks the ability of the communicational conduit to remain open and unproblematic.

Q: Paying attention to the language as object and to the sign as a poetic principle conveys immediacy at the level of reading, even though the context cannot be completed. How do you see a new reformulation of the relationship sing-meaning-experience?

A: One of the biggest changes in literary reception since the avant garde of the teens has been the introduction of the text as activity rather than static totality. The gradual materialization of the sign, oddly enough, has liberated the reader *not* to be a consumer, but a co-producer. A writer like Stein was interested in repetition as a principle that can only be experienced over time. She could work her magic not because all of the parts added up to a discrete "statement" but because the endlessly reconfigured senses of a given phrase (as in "Patriarchal Poetry," for example) would empty that phrase of conventional associations and replace them with the activity of writing. This doesn't mean that writing is unmoored from social or personal statement ("Patriarchal Poetry" is profoundly about masculinist power as manifested in rhetoric), but that if it is to be "true" to its subject, it must be an instance of (and intervention in) that subject.

CARLA HARRYMAN

Photo by Mark Alice Durant

Carla Harryman's poetry can be characterized by those terms she seems most familiar with in **The Middle**, that is, imitation, translation or implication. Any of these concepts are appropriate since her extensive literary production gathers eclectic influences taken from Kathy Acker, Wittgenstein, Georges Bataille or the daily newspaper itself. She disconnects the verb from its subject, the adjective from the noun, she breaks the sentence and, finally, we have to re-compose that puzzle/text full of suggestions and vague impressions that has surely nothing to do with the original composition. Her poetic writings show a stylistic ambivalence, with the paragraph prevailing as a way of approaching the quotidian and with one obsession, as Bob Perelman has pointed out, not to write in the service of any kind of consistent unity. Born in Orange County (CA) in 1952 her most pertinent books are **Percentage** (1979), **Under the Bridge** (1980), **Property** (1982), **The Middle** (1983), **Vice** (1986), **Animal Instincts** (1989), and **In the Mode of** (1991).

Q: In *The Middle* we find a lot of quotations such as those from Creeley, Freud, Kathy Acker, Wittgenstein, Jane Bowles, G. Bataille and George Perec. Do they conform to the authentic background of that middle field you are interested in?

A: Those writers, or perhaps I should say the fragmented passages of writing I used by those writers, participate in the construction of a "dynamic" that might be considered, if you could hold it still, a middle field. I say in the introduction to the **Writing/ Talks** version of "The Middle":

> When I came up with "The Middle" as a title, I didn't know why I chose it. I think it has to do with Jane Austen, whom I never refer to in the text. But she had a sense of balance in all matters, and the middle is contained in this balance. For me, that's not particularly true: the middle is inbetween two extremes, and I keep going back and forth. Actually, if I could just run down the middle of the road and no cars would hit me, I'd be really happy.

Freud was used as a household word or as a location –or as an excuse to localize an examination. The place *Freud* is related to the place *tragedy* –"an interior cosmogeny of fate." Tragedy, when viewed from the perspective of being central to culture, is not an extreme. Same with Freud. When seen from the point of view of an improviser, one who works off the idea that if there is a "center" it is everywhere and where one might choose to move to, or make, or be in and it's also where "you" are and "you" may have never thought about Freud or even about tragedy but possibly something else, Freud might represent an extreme of cultural identity and place –interior.

What is interesting is influence and usage not authenticity. I think of Freud as a kind of concoction, a neo-classical aesthetician, a Victorian scientist and a modernist theoretician. Well, this is imprecise, but an outsider like me i.e. a female, one who provides the "background" or subcentrality to the male –the central figure in Freud– might feel free to create an outsiders vocabulary. And I do not have access to tragedy in the same way because of, for instance, social uses of languages. In one scenario, *Man* is a tragic figure and *women* and *children* are merely victims. In another scenario man is a tragic fixture and women and children are demonic. All of this is a kind of frozen and all-to-powerful ideological hysteria. One might oppose the works of some of those others you mention in your question to these conventional psycho-theoretical polarizations.

A very conflicting experience is that of being taken over by words that one does not think oneself, that one does not wish to agree with, but to be so taken over by the words that any kind of orientation or relationship to those words becomes irrelevant. A salesperson comes to the door and goes away with some money leaving behind a 10 year selection of pink soap. Well, "I would never have bought that," I say. But I did buy it... If I had been wearing a dinosaur mask everything might have turned out differently.

At this point, you might glean that the "middle field" is a construction as opposed to a place of origin.

Q: I've noticed that you prefer partiality to globalization, especially at the level of writing. Can this be seen as a literary or political gesture?

A: "Globalize" is an interesting word because it rings with a tone of technology and thereby is tinted differently than the word "universal." "Globalize" does not call up the solitary figure of genius identifying the essential qualities unique to all humanity, that are really, in fact, *products* of documents like the Rights of Man. Nevertheless, the tint of the word "universal" casts itself shadow-wise upon the odd word, "global."
It is impossible for me to be honest in answering this question because I have too many answers and they are all wrong. I get stuck on "literary" and "political". Perhaps the interest in partiality is "intellectual" and "emotional." I want to apprehend the social/ political content in a configuration that alerts, alarms, teases, plays. This is partially psychological, a construction of understanding that wants to have political meaning .
Vice was more or less written inbetween my child's naps when he was an infant and to a smaller degree at the museum where I worked during ten or fifteen minute breaks. At that time in my life, I either had to learn to write under literally fragmented conditions or forget it. I used everything I could from what I was encountering in daily life. I saved gallery reception invitations for their images; I pillaged art catalogs from work; when I did errands, I'd listen to the car radio and make use of that information. The work is constructed from the experience of having to make do with what I had easy access to, because I had very little time to contemplate otherwise. This is something that also made perfect sense, since there is a plethora of things to think about because there is a plethora of things and thoughts in circulation. So I made the work in the spirit of collision. Whatever I collided into was what I would make use of.
Now, is this political or aesthetic, intellectual, emotional, psychological? The technical constraint on the work are semiautobiographical but the work in itself is not autobiography. It is a method of playing with the conditions of one's life, of seeing that

as possible, I suppose rather than of experiencing some kind of defeat because the conditions are all wrong for what one wants to do. The political and the literary are part of this play.

I am one person. I have one life. My vote no longer, if it ever did, means anything. Sometime other forms of political action do count. But I am only one in the sense of being the producer of literary works. I believe that one person can only do what one person can do and no more. I think that it is dangerous for people to substitute themselves for the fantasized actions of many. I think that one person must perceive herself to be part of many. I am partial in that I can not account for everything. It is interesting that I say this and that one of my favorite authors is Balzac, who wanted to account for everything. It may be impossible to know what the value of being a person or one person among many is. There is no culture for that and therefore no cultural knowledge. The individual looms hugely himself/herself and yet politically unaware. The institutionalized political structure here protects this looming expansiveness of privacy. And yet, this is just a product of ideology, in a world where, in fact, there are many communities with different views of how the individual fits into community. And yet, like individuals, communities are kept to themselves, politically and culturally isolated, unknown in any larger cultural context. The fact of a "larger cultural context" is something like the combination of television and just pure illusion. I keep thinking, "a city is built on a desert." If one thinks of the desert as pervasive, the city is fragile. If one thinks of the city as pervasive, the desert is fragile. If one thinks of the desert as pervasive and the city fragile, one is creating or participating in a kind of animistic creation. If one thinks of the city as pervasive and the desert fragile, one invokes the reality and possibility of destruction. What is the part? Where is the whole? What is in the picture?

Q: You seem to prefer short sentences in most of your books. Do you feel more comfortable in that verbal structure or is it a way of including more polyvalent and semiotic elements?

A: I have always been interested in reduction. I used to think of some of my prose paragraphs as synopsis of non-existent novels. My work is inherently involved in the fronting of words as material. The way words are used in a sentence call attention to the words and the sentence as object. Another influence on my style is the poetic line. When I was younger, I discovered that my attempts at using line breaks were phoney. Yet, I was attracted to the line, the autonomy and interdependence of lines in verse. This also had an effect on the way I use sentences. But it is entirely possible that I already wrote like this before any of this thinking took place and that the thinking about the sentence was involved in the process of inventing a method out of something "I knew already."

Finally, the way I use sentences is involved with discovery. I have rejected certain ideas about centrality. There is not one meaning or finding as I say in **The Middle**, nor is there necessarily a primary story or theme fed by a bunch of sub plots. Nor is there only a cacophony of sounds and jumbled thought. There are other orders by which people think and live by, which I want to call up, find out about. This has something to do with "invisibility." In schools, I notice, younger children's intelligence as it is manifested through language play and body language. There is so much significant knowledge that is ignored in educational institutions. I think that people do not necessarily stop knowing what they know and discovering what they discover on that level, but that certain forms of thinking are simply kept quiet, kept away, kept hidden. There are few locations in a public or social sense to value the creative. It is therefore everywhere hidden.

Q: Unlike other 'language poets' you use a technique that suggests contexts more or less related to each other, how do you conceive your poetics?

A: I do not think of poetics as being identical to the work, but if pressed, I would say that my poetics is oriented around an idea of theatricality. The contexts you suggest are seen as something like social tableau. Language stands in various relationship to what are often unstated contexts, but the contexts also come through because the language is identifying relationship. The theatricality of the language is not necessarily related to normal conventions of 'real' theater, but to an idea of theater. It is this: that a theatrical language is the point where the spoken and the written are inextricably connected. Where writing, for instance, might get turned into an idea about a public, aural act but is still written.

Q: In one of her letters Lyn Hejinian praises your absolute confidence in the control of narrative. Is there a conscious mode regarding that performance?

A: Yes. But absolute control? This is not possible for an improviser.

Q: Your essays insist on the idea of creation. How do you experience the relationship between creation and reality?

A: I write with the idea that I'm making up where the words go. But the idea may be minuscule in the scheme of things and where the words go may seem at times outside the idea. The words are already there. A writing does not attempt to defeat objectivity but to challenge what constitutes objectivity. Literary writing is aware of the construction of "the objective." Writing "creation not reality" is a kind of mock confession.

But creation and reality are words. They have materiality, they invoke other words, associations. My assertion about the creative is more related to the forms of intellectual attachment to the words than it is to issues about realism.

Attachment to representation of reality in writing can be a kind of moralism. When I wrote the statement "creation not reality" in 1979 in **Under the Bridge**, I wanted to challenge what it was that causes writers to defend their work on the basis of realisms. Realism was a kind of exciting topic in the air which did not seem as pertinent to my own project as some might have claimed by fiat –and by association. So "creation not reality" might have been a kind of personal claim raised to a manifesto-like rhetoric. I wanted to experience the effect of the statement.

I am experiencing the effect of the statement now.

One thing I like to do is play with modes of presentation of statement. I could have said the same thing with more explanation, it could have had a diaristic tone, it could have had a scientific tone. It could have referred to past reading on theories of the new novel. It could have been presented as a religious statement, or as a kind of strange political statement. I might have said, "the world is so unacceptable that we have to recreate it." But who are *we* or *the world*? It gets more difficult to say.

I am very attracted to manifestoes, to gestural assertions in art. I have a hard time being very polemical myself, because I am always thinking about how things get put together.

A child draws a picture of bombs and guns. He asks, "I don't like the war, but is it okay to draw these things?"

There is a necessity in creating a tie to the world. The child's picture of bombs is not the same thing as a bomb. The child makes a conquest of a murderous impulse. The impulse is transformed into an image, an image that evokes the power from the world that the child lives with and embodies, or contains. This form of creation is a form of successful containment and transformation.

The image of the bomb is not the bomb. But neither does the bomb exist only in a metaphorical hyperspace. If people in this country could think that the image and reality are not the same thing in some kind of critical way, what would happen?

It is so disgusting to witness helplessly this brainwashing on the media. I received a business letter today that started out celebrating the U.S. victory and then went on with the business at hand. The consensus is invented and then assumed. To many people, this creation of lies, is reality.

Brainwashing is an interesting term that has become reality. At first it was invented by U.S. intelligence to make people believe in the evils of communism. "Communists brainwash." The word did not exist before the U.S. Intelligence's creation of it. Now we see the endless manifestation of brainwashing on our televisions everyday. It has been embraced as a method of social control by U.S. media and government alike. It is creation that has become reality.

Q: What did you intend in *Percentage*? I perceive it as a dialogue reflecting the language of interactions or personal construction of the self...

A: This is an interesting assessment of this play because none of the speeches are contextualized, so it does mimic perhaps that movement of language within one's silent speech that could be called a manifestation of the self; however, it is not interested in identity. There is no dilemma of the self being proposed.

One of the things that I'm interested in, in this play, theatrically, is empty space. I was very curious about what the effect of a work that had no contextualization of dialogue and in which the dialogue did not develop along the lines of character or plot definition, would have on a theatrical space. When there is silence in a narrative play, the silence is narrative too. It supports and adds to the narrative. But in a play like this, the jump or space between each part of the dialogue is more like an object or substance. I wanted to hear the voice liberated from narrative determinates but to allow it speech-like gestures.

The play was also influenced by the study of dance and movement. In studying movement, I discovered that one could disassociate the voice from the body. One could place one's voice-sound at a remove from one's body, spatially, and create a gap. In doing this I started to hear things more gesturally than I had before.

My favorite staging of **Percentage** took place in a large barn-like space in San Francisco. Eileen Corder and I sat in two chairs and looked straight at the audience while we spoke the lines. I conceived this rendition as a movement performance but one in which it was the voice that moved in the space, disassociating from the body, and the body's role was to provide a recurring point of departure for the gestural speech.

Q: What consists of "being imitated by poetry" as you insinuate in *Property*?

A: In **Property** the line goes: "I do not wish to imitate poetry but to be imitated by it." I do not recall a similar statement in **Vice**. I believe this is part of a long monologue in quotations. I have identified the statement "I do not wish to imitate poetry but to be imitated by it", with this rhetorical figure, the uncle. It is a grandiose, theatricalized statement, and could be read in any number of ways. The uncle might be saying that as a subject, he is what should interest poetry. Poetry should be studying him. Given the rather diffuse assignation of character to speeches and monologues in **Property**, one might read this as a kind of style, which has become a character. The style is the self-centered character. And yet the style is only in the writing. There is no character-simulacrum for it to reside in. The non-existent character expresses a desire to be the subject of the poem, as if the poem shaped itself around a human subject. But his words are the poem and the poem does not orient itself around him. In this way, the autonomous-privileged-originator-of-culture type is satirized.

I am interested in the capacity for imitation and its relationship to knowledge. I might say that **Property** imitates characters as if they were words or syntax. If I were, as a self, composed of rhetorical gestures, pedagogical statements, and sincerely contrived metaphors how would I imitate in writing the gestures, statements, and metaphors of which I composed myself? Imitation is a form of play.

LYN HEJINIAN

Photo by Manuel Brito

Lyn Hejinian appears before the eyes of the reader as a poet who shows a special sensibility for the minutest detail or that transitory moment that only she can apprehend. Recollecting "her life" without a chronological control is another way of telling us that our reality is definitively non-conclusive. Sometimes personal experiences disappear leaving no traces but on other occasions we have to exercise our imagination as she opens the door of writing as a way of knowledge. Lyn Hejinian destroys any sense of certainty, she consciously provokes shadows at various levels of meaning, but paradoxically she arouses in us a greater interest in knowing why she stimulates us so much. She prefers to play with lines and paragraphs but, as she says, "language makes us restless...and that restlessness is curiosity or the Faustian rage to know." She was born in San Francisco and attended Harvard University, her bibliography comprises some books that have modified the contemporary poetic scene. Since 1976 she has published books such as **A Thought Is the Bride of What Thinking** (1976), **A Mask of Motion** (1977), **Gesualdo** (1978), **Writing Is an Aid to Memory** (1978), **My Life** (1980), **The Guard** (1984), **The Hunt** (1991), **Oxota: A Short Russian Novel** (1991), and **The Cell** (1992). She also co-authored **Leningrad** (1991). As well as being a leading figure in modern poetry she has also been an editor of Tuumba Press and **Poetics Journal** (1981–), apart from being a gifted translator and an acute essayist.

Q: After living in the mountains and without the modern utilities you integrated yourself in the urban life of the city; how was that process?

A: Urban life requires numerous, various acts of integration and reintegration, more than country life as I experienced it required, not because that country life was uneventful but because events in the quite remote area where my husband, two children, and I were living were themselves integrated –they confirmed each other. There were plenty of adventures –rattle snakes, bears, forest fires, a range war, an escaped prisoner and a cowboy posse pursuing him– but it took very little analysis to respond to them. Urban life, on the other hand, at least in the U.S., where the milieu of the city includes elements from so many and such diverse cultures, is radically self-conscious. One is confronted with perceptual and even with ethical situations that require one to question one's position, quite literally.

The intensification of self-consciousness that our move back to the city occasioned was difficult, as I remember it, and to some extent oppressive. But it resulted, at the same time, in an intensification of the epistemological conditions and investigations from which my poetics and my literary life continue to evolve.

It was in the context of this move –away from the landscape of mountains and ranch lands (what is called chaparral) to that of city streets and social space– that I wrote **Writing Is an Aid to Memory**. I posited a language landscape, with as much specificity as one grants particular rocks, trees, and conditions of sky. I could say then, too, that it was in the context of this work that I made the move to the city.

Of course I didn't simply move generally to the city, but rather I moved at a particular time, July of 1977, to a particular place, the San Francisco Bay Area, and into a situation where literary activities of such as Ron Silliman, Barrett Watten, Rae Armantrout, Tom Mandel, Kit Robinson, Carla Harryman, Steve Benson, Bob Perelman, and I were coinciding. It was a startling situation, and it has deeply informed the process by which I did and do continue to integrate myself on a daily basis into urban life and my life.

Q: Nowadays how do you see your involvement with the literary community of the Bay Area, especially with the people that Hannah Wiener called GROUP MIND?

A: I don't know where or in what context Hannah Wiener used the term 'group mind,' but I'll assume that she meant something like collective consciousness, as distinct from Jung's notion of a collective unconscious. And likewise I'll assume that her 'group mind' is not normative, since that wouldn't be accurate to my experience of the part of the Bay Area literary community to which I belong. In fact, my community is made up of different minds –and by that I don't mean personalities but rather radical processes of being conscious. Though we (I'm referring of course to the so-called language poets but also to poets like Jean Day, Jerry Estrin, and Laura Moriarty whom I got to know in the 80s somewhat after the most intense and intentional period of activity of the 'language school') have in common an emphasis on a poetry of consciousness, the forms that poetry takes are as distinct from one another as the mentalities (psyches) in which our different consciousness are located.

My involvement with the community has not diminished, though it and the community have changed. When I came back to the Bay Area in 1977, my Tuumba Press, Barrett Watten's **This** magazine and **This** press, Bob Perelman's **Hills** magazine and the Talks series he curated, Tom Mandel's **Miam**, Ron Silliman's **Tottel's,** and the weekly reading series at The Grand Piano curated by Ron Silliman, Tom Mandel, and Rae Armantrout were all functioning and doing somewhat in collaboration. Geoff Young's press The Figures was publishing books by many of us. Very shortly thereafter Carla Harryman inaugurated her **Qu** magazine devoted to new prose, and Kit Robinson and I started a weekly live radio show named after his poem 'In the American Tree' and subtitled 'new writing by poets.' This was a period of intense literary activity, as you can imagine, and also of intense social activity. It was, in retrospect, a bohemian scene, one which the current economy simply no longer permits. We had time to talk, argue, read each other's work, and time to read 'secondary' texts from which, or against which, we were elaborating our own common poetics and separate theories.

The climate of the 90s is very different. But what is more relevant, I think, is the fact that our sense of a broad common project developed in such a way as to propel and support what are now different projects. Perhaps that's no more than saying that we've matured as artists. Or that artistic movements have a life span.

Was there a 'movement'? There was no sacrifice of individuality, but rather a radicalizing of the possibilities of individualism. That was not always clear, but it is to me now in retrospect.

The community, as the focus of literary activity, is more disparate now. I think that's appropriate. It's curious that a number of us are, however, working together now on collaborations. Carla and I are writing a picaresque book about eros and sex; Barrett, Ron, Michael Davidson, and I have written a collaboration based on ten days spent together in Leningrad; Kit and I have collaborated (or corresponded) on a project that resulted in **Individuals**, my book **The Cell**, and several long works of Kit's; Ray Di Palma and I have finished a collaboration entitled **Chartings**; and Barrett and I co-edit and publish **Poetics Journal**.

Meanwhile the friendship –intellectual and emotional– is part of my daily life.

Q: Tuumba became a representative series which served as an expounder of the new poetry in the 80s; what was the purpose of editing those fifty books?

A: I founded Tuumba Press because poetry (like anything else) is meaningless without context, without conditions. Literary life in America isn't given, it has to be invented and constructed, and this process of inventing and constructing, as I saw it, was simply an extension of my writing, of my being a poet. Small presses, magazines, poetry readings are the constructs of our literary life and provide conditions for writing's meanings.

I've heard Clark Coolidge muse sometimes over the question, 'What do poets do?' We know that carpenters do, and pilots, and nurses. Providing a milieu for contextualized, unisolated, thinking has got to be a part of what poets can do.

Q: Hegel, Proust, Melville were your favorite authors and you refer to them as writers with a language of quantity, reflective of your own sense of life as dense language. How can this fact be considered in your work?

A: There tends to be some confusion or misconception, inherent maybe to Western thinking, which assumes a separation between, for example, form and content, verb and noun, process and condition, progress and stasis. But in fact these pairs and their parts are a dynamic, a momentum, a force. Quantities are change, not categories. Not accumulations, but gain and loss. By the way, this can be said of gender, too –man and woman. Being a woman isn't a state so much as it's an impetus, with a certain momentum, occurring at various velocities and in various directions.

Or one could speak about literary form, which isn't form at all but force. Thus, for example, Barrett Watten's incredible inventiveness with respect to form in his writing constitutes a series of inventions of motion. These suggest to me new ways to think, new powers of thinking.

It has been years since I read Hegel, and when I did read his work I did so very fantastically. That is, I had reasons for reading Hegel which Hegel would not have anticipated nor approved; and I don't remember what they were. And I don't think I would name 'favorite' authors anymore, unless maybe in the looseness of conversation and deeply contextualized, since anything is favorite in context; favorite-ness is largely a condition of mediation.

Both Proust and Melville are writers of a dense milieu; Gertrude Stein is another. Being a writer, and experiencing experience as dense milieu, I, so to speak, identify with the impulse of these writers –which is to say, they have been an inspiration and an influence for me. The longevity, and the interplay between symmetry and asymmetry, in Proust's and Melville's syntax and in Stein's semantics, much show up in my work. Style is really velocity of thinking in a landscape of thought. With turns. I immensely admire Proust's and Stein's turns. But Proust's great work is a discovery or demonstration of continuities, and my experience also includes radical discontinuities. This is obviously the result of historical conditions, although I don't have any nostalgia for a world of continuities. On the other hand, I don't have fear of it either. But I have talked from time to time in the past about gaps, gaps between sentences, for example, and how one thinks across them. Gaps are sometimes essential to my work, although they don't exclude linkages and turns.

Q: The unconventional poetic prose of *My Life* is composed of many paragraphs and each of them is introduced by a statement or an insinuation; to what degree are they influenced by those readings of Proust or of Mandelstam?

A: I've been responding to these questions one day at a time, and I arrive at this one only a few hours after learning that the U.S., along with England, Saudi Arabia, and Kuwait, has attacked Iraq. I can't resolve such information, not by forgetting it and not by aestheticizing it. I am stunned, and then surprised by terrible and intense feelings of grief and fear –not a grand fear but rather a small fear, resembling furtiveness. War is under scrutiny by this grief and fear; but it's the subject, not the object, of that scrutiny. In this sense, it refuses abstraction; it forms into innumerable particulars.
In some respects, my emotional response resembles my feelings toward death, the deaths of certain people I've loved and, in

fact, continue to love, and especially to the death of my father. (In thinking about this war, I also recognize something virtually identical to my abhorrence of the death penalty.)

I can say that **My Life**, apart from technical concerns (the exploration of the long and short sentences, of parataxis, of the varieties of metonymic associating or metonymic logics, of social and familial speech as mental fact, of repetition and change, etc.), was motivated by a fear of death, or by the anticipation of loss. And it is in this that I feel an affinity with Proust, whose astonishing style is a representation of the tension between momentum and lingering that a mind, wanting always to be conscious that it's alive, experiences.

What is sad and frightening about a person's death (even the deaths of young soldiers in war) is only partially the loss of that person's future –what he or she might have seen or done. Much worse is the loss of that person's past, of his or her memory and thus of his or her experience, the obliteration of the emotional intellect in which enormous intensities of response radiate and in which the fabric of the significance of everything has been woven exists. It's the loss of having lived.

Last night, I was looking through **Remembrance of Time Past** in anticipation of answering your question (in a very different way from what is emerging today), to find the phrase from which the opening pre-text of **My Life** ('A pause, a rose, something on paper') was (metonymically) translated. I didn't find it readily and was impatient so I didn't look long. It is in a description of an approach to Combray, which the narrator sees emerging from the distance, bit by bit suffuses with what he knows: the plain, the spire, a radiance anticipating the color of the streets. Something like that. Proust's style of accretion, of accumulation, meditation, and release (release into consciousness and as such *into the book*) was and is inspiring to me. As 'But when from a long-distance past nothing subsists, after the people are dead, after the things are broken and scattered, still, alone, more fragile, but with more vitality, more unsubstantial, more persistent, more faithful, the smell and taste of things remain poised a long time, like souls, ready to remind us, waiting and hoping for their moment, amid the ruins of all the rest; and bear unfaltering, in the tiny and almost impalpable drop of their essence, the vast structure of recollection.'

By the way, Proust's early literary work (maybe even his first) was a translation of John Rushkin's **The Bible of Amiens**, and under the influence of Rushkin's prose style, Proust developed his own. Rushkin's prose is the result and complex reflection of an obsession with particulars and the ramifications of particulars. This was not a Victorian interest in things but an epistemological one, from which he developed his radical (and some would say eccentric) social politics, one that coincided at many points what Marx's. Rushkin's style was thus a representation of privilege. I admire Rushkin and his writings very much.

Meanwhile, my reading of Gertrude Stein's studies of time and space have amplified what Proust's have contributed to my own sense of those dimensions. And her phenomenology –her rejection of memory as a medium of perception– and the command, 'Begin again,' are vital contradictions to Proust's. It is critical to think and work with contradictions. Or it is typical (of our times) to do so.

Now I should say, by the way, that the 'poetic prose' of **My Life** is highly conventional (and this not 'unconventional' as the question has it). The book as a whole is organized according to structural conventions which I invented in advance and imposed on the writing. There are, in fact, two published versions of the book, one written when I was 37 years old (and published by Burning Deck) and the other revised when I was 45 (and published by Sun and Moon Press). The first has 37 paragraphs, of 37 sentences each, and the latter has an additional 8 paragraphs (making 45) and 8 new sentences were added to the original 37 paragraphs. In other words, the later version consists of 45 paragraphs with 45 sentences in each. In addition, every paragraph (or poem) is preceded by a sentence or phrase, one which subsequently is repeated (though sometimes slightly altered), suggesting the recurrence and recontextualization of what I think and of what I know.

Meanwhile, conventional language is pervasive throughout the book –cliches ('Pretty is as pretty does'), turns of phrase typical of my social milieu ('I've got a big day tomorrow'), idiosyncratic witticisms of my relatives ('cottage fromage,' 'I've had a peachy time), metaphors embedded in the American language ('to take a vacation,' 'to spend some time'). The book is about the formative impact of language, and at the same time it is a critique of that language –suggesting that one can construct alternative views. **My Life** is both determined and constructed. My life, too.

This is a milieu, of course, of contradiction.

But not of opposites. I don't believe in opposites.

The question mentions Osip Mandelstam. The Soviet period of Russian literature is one which is absolutely wild with contradiction and with contrary impulses –most obviously, for example, toward East and West, toward the educated and the massive, toward individual expression and social utility. And so forth. Mandelstam is one of the great writers of this period, and I admire his work very much. But I don't think he has exerted much influence on my own writing.

I apologize for burdening my response to this question with comments about war. Recent events are extraneous to these questions, but context is crucial to their answers. That, finally, is what I have wanted to 'get at' –the context of consciousness and the consciousness of context.

Q: At the College of Arts and Crafts (in 1978) you gave "the students work with language situations, translations, transformations, numerical equivalency systems, random configurations, transition processes..." This seems to be a declaration of your poetics...

A: I'm writing out my responses to these questions in Canada, from a large arts school and theater center in a quite small town in the Canadian Rockies, where around 100 art students and artists are studying or working. People are watching the war news on television, usually over the cable news station CNN. The room where the television sits isn't big –it's very warm there because so many people are in the room. There is absolutely no conversation. We have been listening to any possible news of the missile attack on Israel and what Israel's response will be. Usually in a crisis people, even strangers, talk to each other –for reassurance, and to build up the comradeship that one might have to depend on in case of need. Here artists from many countries are watching news of the beginning of war in complete silence, isolated from each other. I don't know why.

The atmosphere in the room with the tv resembles that of a railroad or bus depot. No one stays for long in the room, people come and go wearing their coats and boots, a stranger passing among strangers, perhaps absorbing the news privately.

1978, when I taught at the California College of Arts and Crafts, wasn't so very long after the end of the Vietnam War –a war that was never declared to be such in the United States. A major component of my poetics, or let's say of my poetic impulse, is a result of that war and the meaning of its never being named.

But as for the question –in fact the assignment to work with 'language situations, translations,' and so forth was not primarily a manifestation of my poetics, although I certainly wanted to suggest to the students, and to help them discover, that systems and structures are also ways of thinking, a means for interpretation, of going from one thing to another and beyond one's expectations. But my assignments were also intended to encourage the students to write work that wasn't an expression of their anguished egos. It was a difficult class, because not a single student had any interest in being a writer. In order to get a degree at CCAC every student had to take a certain number of Humanities courses, and a 'poetry writing' course looked like an easy way out. There was one student, a man named Michael McCabe, who was extremely inventive and intelligent. But some of the others presented me with very real problems by writing *to* me about very private and in two cases disturbing matters, which I hadn't the training or the inclination to deal with. My solution was to force them out of themselves and into more social aspects of language –the systems interwoven through it that make it comprehensible to its users, the structures that make it a framework and constraint on knowledge, some ways of distorting syntax to arrive at unexpected fields of meanings, and so forth.

I was using such things to develop my own thinking at the time, too. I've never taught material that was entirely under my control and completely out of the control of my students.

But except for the logical, almost elegant, formula that provides the superstructure for **My Life** I've never discovered or invented a number system that satisfied me as a metaphor, or excuse, for a particular piece of writing. I feel as if I am looking for divine guidance, or divine justification, when I do so. I gratefully envy Ron Silliman's use of the Fibonacci series, which provides

Tjanting, for example, with at least natural guidance and justification. It's perfect. It would be redundant for me to do something similar.

One of the benefits of formal devices is that they increase the palpability, the perceptibility of the work. And another is that they can be used to increase the semantic possibilities of a work. Kit Robinson's work provides great (and for me influential) examples of both. Or, Louis Zukofsky's. His five-word lines often leave very odd words at the end of a line, producing lines with no resolution, no way to stop, but the logic slides, the lines reemerge. It's beautiful.

Q: In your correspondence archived at UCSD you appear to be attached to discovering the inner nature of concepts like collage, subjectivity/objectivity, restlessness or the Faustian "rage to know..." and this reminds me a line from *Writing Is an Aid to Memory*: "I am impatient to finish in order to begin..."

A: I had in the past (prior to 1978) used the term *collage* loosely and generally to refer to all art works created or assembled out of diverse materials —works of art emphasizing contiguity, contingency, juxtaposition, realignment, relationship, unlikely pairings, etc. The problem with the term, as I saw when I became more precise, is that it suggests (or can suggest) an unmotivated or unnecessitated groupings of materials. Things are like letters of the alphabet —when you put some of them together they will always appear to be seeking meaning, or even to be making it. The term *montage*, as it was used by and in the tradition of Sergei Eisenstein, seemed better. All the above values were maintained (contiguity, contingency, etc.), but the result reflected decision more than happy chance.

Also *collage* is a predominantly spatial technique, whereas *montage* employs devices that are related to time. In this sense *montage* preserves its nature as a process.

I don't know how to explicate the line 'I am impatient to finish in order to begin...' in terms of an uneasiness with the inadequacies of *collage*, except perhaps to say that the line obviously expresses a certain mental state, impatience, or restlessness, an urge not to stand still, while at the same time it assumes that there's no progressing continuum in which *I* can participate. This mental state could be seen as compulsive, that is, relentlessly aware of possibilities and constraints. Of freedoms and boundary lines.

Q: *The Grreat Adventure* is a diverse book demanding different approaches; there we have the presence of Balzac, Jane Austen... It's also like a notebook (activity instructions, required readings, the questionnaires sent off by balloons). Is non-linearity per se the goal of the book?

A: *Here* is an example of collage.

There are very, very few copies of this *book* in existence –I burned almost all of them.

That is not to say that I renounce the book, or even that I want to distance myself from it. Maybe it would be nice to have had a pure history, but to do so I would have had to have had from an early age of vision of the future. An agenda. An intended trajectory.

But on the contrary, I've been influenced by anything. I don't think non-linearity was the goal of **The Grreat Adventure**; I think it was a summons to impressionability.

Q: The forty-two sections of *Writing Is an Aid to Memory*

are characterized by a subjugate beat, almost a prophetic beat at the level of sound; do you agree with this?

A: I'm assuming that you mean *subjunctive* when you use the word subjugate. If so, this is a very interesting comment. I think the syntax (and its sounds) do set up a field of contingency and provisionality, although I would have said that the work expresses desires (that and other visions) rather than prophesies. I don't have a copy of the book with me, and I don't trust my memory enough to quote without its aid. But the momentum of the cadence, with its departures within arrivals and arrivals and within departures, was intended to push time in both directions, *backward* toward memory and also forward toward *writing*, which is always (for me) indicative of future unforeseen meanings and events. Writing gives one something to remember.

But you refer specifically to a *prophetic* beat, maybe suggestive of solemnity and sphinx-like ambiguity. Truths hidden until found. In such a case, prophecies don't foretell the future, they announce fate. And they are proven, not on criteria established in the future, but on the grounds of memory, in which are displayed the patterns of incident and decision that would lead *inevitably* to the accomplishment of fate. A sense of fate is a result of a retrospective experiencing of experience –an apparent discovery of what was and why it worked. But it depends also on belief in a sublime causality, in a transcendental continuum which I simply can't see. I do believe in irrevocability, but not in fate.

Q: Is there in your poetry an intimate association between line and thought?

A: I think the term *perception* should be added to the configuration, if only in recognition of the world with which line and thought share time and place. I say this because I would like to undermine the opposition between inside and outside in a poem. Although I have varied the shape and quality of lines so as to make each line equivalent to a *unit of thought* or *unit of cognition*, it isn't that the line *contains* the thought, it's rather that it's a possible measure of the activity of thinking within the thinkable, perceivable, world.

Line length and line break can alter perceptual processes in innumerable ways, for both writer and reader. Retardation, flicker, recombination, the extension of speed, immobilization, and myriad other effects are dependent on qualities of line.

And of course thoughts don't occur in divisions, in fact the experience of thinking is more one of combination. So while a line may isolate stages of thought it may also multiply and strengthen the connections in which thought emerges. This occurs especially when line and sentence don't coincide, where the end of one sentence and the beginning of another may combine in a single line.

Q: How did you solve the escape from sentence to paragraph?

A: There was a point in the early 80s, around the time that Ron Silliman was presenting an early version of his essay "The New Essay" as a talk in San Francisco, when I was finding the sentence extremely limiting and even claustrophobic. I hoped that I could open its terminal points (the capital at the beginning and the full stop (period) at the end) by writing in paragraphs, so that sentences were occurring in groups, opening into each other, altering each other, and in every way escaping the isolation and *completeness* of the sentence. But it wasn't until I returned to writing in lines, where I could open up the syntax of sentences from within by setting in motion the syntax of lines at the same time (for example by breaking sentences into two or more lines), that I *escaped*, as you quite perfectly put it, from prose to poetry. **The Guard** is probably a good example of the result.

For the last few years I've been writing sentence-based (rather than a sentence-subverting or sentence-distorting) lines, as for example in **The Cell** and in **The Hunt** which is to be published by Zasterle Press.

In **The Hunt** I think this may reflect a concern with the velocity of experience, or with the experiencing of experience, rather than with meaning per se. The work is a long accounting of, and meditation on, the experience and effect of a number of long and short periods I have spent in Russia. The Zasterle Press version is Book Five of the complete work, which has the same title **The Hunt** (or its Russian equivalent, *Oxota*) and is subtitled *A Short Russian Novel*. It's written in 14-line stanzas (or chapters) in homage to the first great Russian novel, Pushkin's **Evgeny Onegin**, which was subtitled *a novel in verse*. But in order to allow for digressive, anecdotal, common, quotidian, or discursive materials as I heard and observed them, I needed a very flexible line, and a prosaic line –the sentence.

Q: Your poetry is an exploration in language mainly through the sentence and paragraph; what kind of change are you pursuing with this new adopted value?

A: Carla Harryman, Ron Silliman, and Barrett Watten have all used the paragraph as a device, either to organize or to revolutionize (Carla often does this) a text, but I really have not –I could say I have failed to do so. **My Life** is written in sentences, not in paragraphs. And the prose in Carla Harryman's and my ongoing collaboration, **The Wide Road**, uses paragraphs less for themselves than for what can be bound in and released from them; the paragraphs in that work contain various kinds of materials and aren't constructed for the conventional purpose of controlling tone or furthering plot. Each paragraph is a small plot, in a realm of erotically plotted fields –I suppose I could say something like that.

My major goal has been to escape *within* the sentence, to make an enormous sentence –not necessarily long ones, but capacious ones. Somewhat paradoxically, I sometimes try to create this capacity with different compressive techniques –metonymy is the most consistent form of *logic* in my writing. But sometimes long, convoluted sentences from which many conditional clauses depend are instances, for me, of intense accuracy, of a direct route.

But am I, in my sentences (and my use of lines to expand their capacity and accuracy), in pursuit of change? Do I want to improve the world?

Of course. If so, it will have to be *in* sentences, not by them. The sentence is a medium of arrivals and departures, a medium of inquiry, discovery, and acknowledgement.

Q: I think that in *The Guard* privacy is one of the essential elements within the book; is it a dialogue between you and the same text?

A: **The Guard** was written just after my first trip to the Soviet Union, and it's dedicated to Arkadii Dragomoshchenko, the Leningrad poet whom I met for the first time on that trip, and with whom I've been collaborating on various translations and projects since. Contrary to seeking a realm for privacy, the book is about words (those projectiles of communication). It's

words who are guards. And users of words. Do they guard us
or do they guard their things? And are they keeping something
in or something out?

The poem is the result of my first encounter with the Russian
language and also with the disorientation and longing associated
with all my numerous trips to Russia. A similar disorientation
and longing informs much of my writing, or at least I formulated
this rhyme between the two realms of experience, the Russian
realm and the realm of the words for things, when I wrote **The
Guard**.

But beginning to learn Russian did not give me my first or only
experience of the word as an adamant entity. Words have often
had a palpable quality for me, with porosity but not transparency,
productive but unstable. I could imagine a word as a rock; the
rock in a gate; the gate opening but would one say into or out
of some place that *I* enters (Russia) or the first scene in a
landscape encountered on a Dantesque journey to *paradise*
–which is the last word in the poem?

The Guard is about attempted communication, nor privacy.
Maybe we're stuck in privacy, nonetheless. My early attempts
to speak Russian should have made me think so.

Q: Is there any discipline for reading *Individuals*?

A: No, not at all. Kit Robinson and I each wrote twelve of the
twenty-four poems in the book. Kit has taught poetry-writing
in many situations, to young children, to adolescents, to college
students from many areas of society, and he has often said that
the only readers and writers who are blind to the many
dimensions possible in poetry are the overly-trained and overly-
educated. My experience teaching has been the same. The only
qualities necessary for reading and enjoying and learning from

poetry are curiosity and confidence in the possibilities of something's being new and interesting.

The poems in **Individuals** are the result of looking at very ordinary objects and experiences. They are about our respective appreciation for the existence of these things, and for the available strangeness which allows us to know them again and again as if for the first time and yet without having forgotten.

FANNY HOWE

Photo by Manuel Brito

Memory, nature, marriage, soul, time. To see and to hear and one obsession: to return to those early voices such as Keats, Dickinson, Yeats, Thomas, that is, to the great voices all poets are linked to or face in tension. Fanny Howe experiments with all those terms and some autobiographical elements are transmuted into some of her characters. So the final impression goes from the merely personal into something more mythologized. Needless to say, creativity in this author transcends the physical materiality of the event itself and suggests in some of her texts the connection between literary creation and God's creation of earth. Perhaps her New England context made her a poet looking for a synthesis of the inner and outer worlds, a new disposition of home and the world. Educated at Stanford University, she is not only a poet but also a fiction writer. Her literary production comprises books such as **Eggs, The Amerindian Coastline Poem, Poem for a Single Pallet, Alsace Lorraine** (1982), **For Erato: The Meaning of Life** (1984), **In the Middle of Nowhere** (1984), **Introduction to the World** (1986), **Robeson Street** (1985), **Holy Smoke,** and **Sic** (1988).

Q: How do you see yourself writing poems disclosing intimities in an age where materiality and non-discursive approach are prevalent in today poetry?

A: I suppose I'm a lyric poet and unreconstructed adolescent because my expressive impulse is direct –to the world right after I experience it. Yet I believe I live in an age where the transcendent is just as available as it always was. When I had the impulses and beliefs of a materialist, in my twenties, I was in despair. Now I'm older and have been converted into something which attempts to bridge the air between materialism and a spirit life. And I am not at the mercy of a despair, which nonetheless seeks me out, as it does all of us. Despair is the Satan of our time; it is also the partner of cynicism which occupies the hearts of many world leaders, of industrialists and high tech business people –those who are ruining everyone else's time. Thomas Aquinas said that the intellect is useful, but faith and the will are liberating. It seems to me that liberation is the state we long for and that reason can be the most oppressive operative around. We have very reasonable men –nerds– calling the shots and determining the value of our hours as workers; they are by and large cynical and servants of despair. Their materialism is not something I choose to aspire to. As a poet and writer I yearn away from them and try to clarify another set of terms.

Q: The homogeneous succession of paragraphs is constantly present in your fiction and sometimes in your poetry, do you consider them an essential fact in your work?

A: The way I block out my writing is an acknowledgement of the overwhelming presence of silence. It is indeed essential to the balancing of what is recorded with what is inexpressible.

Q: In your correspondence you mention a desire for returning to these voices: Keats, Dickinson, Yeats, and Thomas and also for discovering the great voice, would you explain this?

A: When I was young and full of hope I fell in love with poetry. The first poets I read at that time –from a little anthology of world poetry, all in translation– included Li Po, Akhmatova, Pushkin, Catullus and many others. Later I became a student of French literature and Baudelaire was my favorite. Shakespeare was of course everywhere around, and I think the difficulty I had in grasping his meanings, while I was loving his soundings, became the difficulty that drove me to write poetry. I think people seek the greatest difficulty they can, and for me poetry is just that.

Q: I think that many of your poems can be linked to an Emersonian Transcendentalism, particularly at the level of apprehending the relationship of the common things and their spiritual perception...

A: The fact that I come from New England with a sort of Emersonian Transcendentalist streak makes it seem like a genetic fate. But of course, as a Catholic convert, I have developed a

more incarnational theology than Emerson's. I feel that we are
already occupying divine territory, on earth, and that we can't
escape it once we are consciously in it. The Buddhists are the
most enlightened purveyors of the experienced of being *in
heaven* –of *God* as experience, rather than object– but I feel no
contradiction between their expression of enlightenment and
the traditional Western doctrine of incarnation.

**Q: There's an evident preoccupation in your poems for the
ordinary things of the city life, especially for its sordid
environment, but everything is involved in an ambivalent
concept of time, what is the role of time and its staticism
in your creative writing?**

A: My concept of time is always changing, but I keep returning
to the sense that time is simultaneous, and all exists now, in the
form that Blake presents in his theology. I figure we are intended
to experience time exactly as we do, even if it is *wrong*, because
it is the only way we can measure the value and meaning of
our actions here. This is where I link letters and sentences with
time; they are analogous to minutes and hours and aspire to a
justice which is also analogous to our quest for the promised
land. We live out our sentence in a world which is more
absolutely unjust that it is anything else. Except good. It is
more good than it is unjust. And even though we know we
cannot end suffering, our assignment is to combat it. That I
think is the final, most stunning realization I have had –that
everything we do, which is of the most profound value, is
doomed in the short run. But ghosts return –the ghosts of those
who were wronged– one by one– in the course of history.

Q: You said that "the taking of language from outside heralded a further loss of myself." In spite of this confrontation between inner world and outer world, I suspect that you pursue a synthesis in both of them...

A: I want to say that the language poets, to me, perform the critical function of putting words into a verbal landscape without judgement (content) which renders the words equal. This equality becomes the essence of innocence. I admire this work a great deal and really regret that I am –due to temperament– unable to free myself from the charged vocabulary of a romantic. The one way we are equal is in our innocence; if a poetics of materialism makes this clear, it is serving an invaluable function. My politics are, I believe, similar to theirs, which is what creates a bond in spite of aesthetic (or temperamental) differences.

Q: The implicit discourse of your work makes the reader feel oppressive, are we really the victims or the lost ones?

A: Midway through my life, so to speak, I chose to break away from a Freudian and psychoanalytic vocabulary to one which seemed to me (and still does more liberating. This was the vocabulary of theology. Certain contemporary theologians have been trained in existentialist thought and this is reflected in much new writing on the human condition; their thinking is far from naive. Nonetheless they use words which have a resonance which is sweet. A person can be freed and charged with joy by such words. I believe that freedom is the quality all people aspire to, in whatever form it comes to them, according to their circumstances. I mean by freedom a lightness, a sense of relationship to nature and society which is balanced and nondominating, a comfort with one's own and one's neighbor's body which makes waking and walking a pleasure, a way of understanding and being understood which is like a coming home. And of course freedom involves a fearless relationship to silence. As long as we lack such freedom, we are not so much lost, or victimized, as subject to the judgements of our cells.

Q: The concept of sin is the ignorance?

A: Sin, as I understand, or experience it, is the state of being separate from one's original source. Therefore each human is automatically in a state of sin, at birth. The distance between that source increases with age, naturally, lifting the child further and further away from it, and into an adult life where the state of sin is increased voluntarily, by certain unhappy actions. Laws are intended to prevent such slippage, but then they become judgements and infringements on the potential for living close to the source, too. Original sin just acknowledges the fact that human beings suffer. I think Blake has many of the answers.

Q: In the *Amerindian Coast-Line* we have the recurrence of images like cell, jail and house along with other images belonging to nature such as space, ice, and mind. How would you analyze them?

A: I really don't write symbolically, and I hate myths, so when I use images like cell, jail and ice, it is in a spirit of over-excited emotional identification. Again, the sense of incarnation is overwhelming to me. I may be more allegorical, if I understand the term correctly, than anything else, in my use images. To live two lives —one material, the other immaterial— is to live nervously.

Q: You say in *Introduction to the World* "like women/ look new in the court of God." Which are the characteristics of that new look?

A: I am uneasy with the sight of women who have adopted the uniforms of power-like turned-around collars and business suits for Wall Street. I thought the point of our struggle was to denounce the icons of masculine power, not to subsume them. Passive resistance, as practiced by Martin Luther King and Gandhi among others, is probably my model for approaching the power-fields. It is critical that we totally undermine the attributes of the powerful by non-participation in their systems.

Q: The ten luxuries that appear in *Poems from a Single Pallet* (capital, job, car, summer vacation, fear, therapist, peace, good sex, opiate, poetry) seem to be the ten commandments of our age...

A: In this country the sense of entitlement has been inflicted on all its citizens so that the relation to luxuries becomes a kind of commandment from the society, a hidden imperative. The story about rich and poor has lost its sting, since rich and poor change places very casually in the USA. The new narrative, politically, is about cynics and innocents. The cynics turn the named luxuries into commandments which they then punish the others for failing to acquire, Cynicism is the opium of the government which now has colonized its own people.

MICHAEL PALMER

Photo by Manuel Brito

The letter you find as answering my questionnaire emphasizes Michael Palmer's deepest belief: poetry "as part of life." In this sense, its transformation through language is exposed because of his primary interest in Wittgenstein, his use of dance as a poetic metaphor and a literal strategy inside this entity that permits poetry to receive "objects" from different poets. Palmer was born in New York in 1943 and was educated at Harvard University. Among his publications in verse I have to mention **Plan of the City of O** (1971), **Blake's Newton** (1972), **C's Songs** (1973), **Six Poems** (1973), **The Circular Gates** (1974), **Without Music** (1977), **Alogon** (1980), **Notes for Echo Lake** (1981), **First Figure** (1984) and **Sun** (1988). He has been the editor of **Code of Signals: Recent Writings in Poetics** (1983).

22 april 91

Dear Manuel,

Your questions led me to any number of aborted responses and strategies (games) of response, all of them either masking the work or else bathing it in a particular light. I don't want to make any case for the work or posit intellectual substance. Whatever its relation or lack thereof to poststructuralist and later thought is more the business of academicians –is in fact quite literally the "business" of academicians. The rest, its logics and dislogics, its thematic coherence &/or rupture, I'm afraid I've already too much discussed, to the detriment of possible readings, possible meanings.

"We" have just "successfully" bombed the birthplace of written language, treating the desert and its people as a testing ground for the technology of annihilation. On the so-called home front, people have been subjected to a new (old) rhetoric of disinformation, a virtual circus of empty signifiers on white horses. Another chapter added to the century of modernism, whose other chapters cannot be said to be less dark. In that dark we try to read and to somehow respond with letters, words and sentences of our own. Many of these letters have broken apart; many of the words are missing some letters and are unpronounceable; and many of the sentences are unrecognizable as such. Lamentation and celebration can be curiously proximate, as loss to desire, silence to speech.

I hate increasingly the conceit of "artfulness," whether that be taken as acculturated aestheticism or vanguard gesturalism. Yet the noise we make —sometimes a music— can be heard as purposive, as a kind of resistance to meaning as such, or to civilization as such. For years I carried Holderlin's mantra for poetry in my ear, "It is not powerful, but it is part of life." Yet I wonder if the inversion of this might equally hold, since it —poetry— is oddly powerful and insistent, yet hardly a part of life in our time. All the more reason then.

My best,

Michael

Michael Palmer

JEROME ROTHENBERG

Of all the poets included in this book, Jerome Rothenberg is the most "classical" writer among these contemporary authors. Not in vain does his literary career date back to the late fifties. He is the founder of "Ethnopoetics" and developed a theory around concepts such as "deep image". He is a poet who tries to contemporanize any artistic/literary model belonging to any culture. He constantly affirms that the physical senses of human beings exist in order to experiment in an intuitive way but also to stay open to new languages. If we attend his poetical readings we understand instantly why we can't elude the oralities of some poetries. It's impossible to speak succinctly about the importance of this poet. He is always reflecting, looking for and finding those old or anti-canonic poetic forms seemingly obsolete that he re-anthropologizes and makes pertinent to all of us. He was born in New York in 1931 and took his M.A. from the University of Michigan. Currently he is Professor of Visual Arts and Literature at the University of California, San Diego. His bibliography is so extensive that it would exceed this short introductory space. In order to appreciate a comprehensive overview of his bibliography I remit you to the Harry Polkinhorn edition of **Jerome Rothenberg: A Descriptive Bibliography** (1988). His edition of **Technicians of the Sacred: A Range of Poetries from Africa, America, Asia & Oceania** meant a change in current from the always Western centered literary paradigm and gave way to the inclusion of other literatures and ways of writing. He has written around fifty books of poetry always characterized by his sense of renewal and transformation. If I had to mention three definitive books that show his different poetic trends, I'd include **Poland/1931** (1969), **That Dada Strain** (1983) and **Khurbn & Other Poems** (1989) because they represent his very own particular mythology characterized by his Jewishness, his interest in Dadaism and oralism.

Q: You seem a very complex poet. We can observe in your poetry a universe characterized by its relations with myth and history, and in *The Postmoderns*, edited by Donald Allen and George Butterick, you speak about your interest in a simultaneity of ages, places, discoveries, and witnessings that defines Man as a species...

A: Yeah, in that sense I think of myself, if the term still holds, as a *modern*, even a *modernist* poet, an experimental poet, and I don't think of that modernism, as it's sometimes given back to us by those outside it, essentially, a process of disintegration, a poetic psychosis so to speak. My concern has been with a constructive or constructivist modernism that has opened up the possibility of going beyond ourselves as poets. I we start out by deconstructing (a term I'd like to borrow), I continue to have an optimistic view –that poetry isn't merely a record of our fragmentation as a species or our alienation, although that has to enter it too as part of the common experience. Rather, certain advances in our ideas of language or of what a poem is and can contain appear for our use, as sometimes similar and sometimes very different ideas did in the ambition of a Pound or of an Olson, say, to find a way of constructing a new, large work as a kind of a comparatist poetics. I think of myself as really a very different poet from either of those two, & yet I have no trouble at this point to consider myself as sharing an idea of poetry, an overall sense of a new & still developing poetics with a great number of twentieth-century poets, from American & Europe & other places in the world. It seemed to me at an early point –& this is what led directly to the idea of an ethnopoetics– that an opportunity that was given to us as poets in a time of change was not only to create this new work out of a whole cloth, to begin it strictly from ourselves, but to look as well to other cultures, other worlds that had been opened up to us by circumstances of imperialism, by new technologies of travel & communication, by the world becoming smaller, smaller in the process. It was our inheritance, our opportunity to be able to get a truer sense of how language has been used toward poetic ends in a wide range of cultures. So we have the chance to see what poetry is, what it might come to be in the future, in part because the past –the idea of, the contents of the past– is more & more available to us. I found that realization, when it came to me, was a thing of great excitement.

Q: Which years do you refer to?

A: Well, I think it was a part of the post-World War II awareness. It must have been one of those attitudes encouraged by the war, or in its aftermath. An attitude toward boundaries –national, cultural, & ethnic– that we found to be stultifying and acting against the fuller realization of what we were or could be. It pretty much pulled us away from nationalism, & yet it coincided with a period of intense American chauvinism, with a feeling that we had come at last & forever into the great American moment, that our art, poetry, music were suddenly thrust forward, were now a center of attention. The dominance of American power puts a lot of what we want as poets into doubt, in part because we enjoy playing that central role,

although it blinds us, *even us*, to the greater human *being* that
has opened up before us. So there's room there for both optimism
& despair.

**Q: I think that this fact can be clearly seen in *A Big Jewish
Book*, where you added some notes on the sources of
selections and related materials. Is there an intent to be the
man/poet who approaches wisdom and at the same time
searches for the discovery of origins?**

A: But I would be careful not to connect the search for origins
too closely with the **Jewish Book**. The same search goes on in
the other books, from **Technicians of the Sacred** on. And I
have trouble with that other term as well –a mixed attitude
shared with others toward what Olson called "*wisdom as such.*"
He proposed himself to be against that in Duncan's work, &
I'm not sure if I share that attitude or not. But there's definitely
a concern all around with *origins* –like the fact that Cid
Corman's magazine which was so early into Olson & the rest
was titled **Origin**. I want above all to be clear about the word
origin as it relates to **A Big Jewish Book**, because given that
title one can take it, in current American terms, as being a
personal ethnic search for Jewish origins. To me that's somewhat
off the point. The process that began for me with **Technicians
of the Sacred** was a search for human origins, for the common
and uncommon ground between the world's cultures, including
very much those cultures that had been endangered in this time,
this century. These were cultures that contained not only a
tremendous amount of human wisdom *as such*, but very useful,
very fruitful forms of human imagination, ways of structuring
& restructuring reality through language. So what I had in front
of me was the possibility of seeming to go backwards, to

explore those things –those traditions, oral & other– as they may have developed in this or that culture. In **A Big Jewish Book** I chose specifically to focus on that complex of traditions –not single tradition but a complex of traditions– that might come together under a single designating term like *Jewish*. Part of the attraction was that I could enter into it as a direct participant in a way that I couldn't, say, with the American Indian poetry. With the Native Americans there was always the sense of being the outsider looking in on it, you know, perhaps intruding on it, interfering with it, doing perhaps a certain amount of harm, however much one tried to do a little bit of good. With **A Jewish Book**, I felt that anything I did was from the inside. I also felt that the Jewish anthology as such –that kind of ethnically centered configuration– was itself a debased form, but a form that had, if one went at it in a total way, all sorts of lovely possibilities. It seemed to me that it could be something richer & more complex than it had previously been made to be. I think I also did it when I did out of a certain feeling of frustration. I regretted when I was through with **Technicians of the Sacred** that it had had no European section, although I wasn't about to launch a huge European anthology as a way of compensating. But since the fate of the Jews was so much tied into the history of Europe, since the Jews through diaspora had gone into so many places & adapted themselves to so many languages & cultures, it seemed to me that the resultant Jewish complexity reflected in its special way a larger world complexity. In this way, then, the Jewish book was a substitute for the large European anthology, & throughout I felt a real excitement in putting it together, in being able to discover examples of poetry that resembled but diverged sharply from what I knew as European –forms of poetry that I had previously not imagined to have existed. All kinds of language constructs, poems built on numerological principles, & so on, appeared to me through this investigation of Jewish poetry across the board. That's something I've continued to pursue –that there was a verbal/visual tradition, a sense of language & reality, that went very far back; the idea of language as an instrument in forming (as well as describing/mapping) the entire universe, the possibility of describing reality itself through the elemental or constituent forms of language, the relation that this assumes between the alphabet & the structure of the world as such. And I guess it's for this reason that Einstein's formulation $E = mc^2$ is presented in **A Big Jewish Book** as a kind of highly compressed poem...

Q: ...But not only this conversion of Einstein's formulation into poetry. You say in the section, "*Work of Creation*," that "*all numbers and all sounds converge.*"

A: The Einstein was my single scientific *example*, seeing that as an act of poesis, & I certainly didn't want to belabor the point by including a whole series of such equations. Putting one such equation into that particular context (of language & reality: a universe of letters & of numbers) was enough. That sentence in my "*Work of Creation*" relates more closely, anyway, to a *musical* concept of numbers (in terms of measure, a *poetic* one). At a certain point in human history, the same kind of imagination that was creating a mathematics was also creating –in formal terms– a music. So the relation between music & mathematics seems very close. In poetry, which also opens other avenues of meaning, there's an inherent music –of the metrics & the measure– in what was spoken of traditionally as *numbers*. To write in numbers meant in English that you wrote in metered language, as when Alexander Pope, boasting of his ability as a small child, says: "*I lisp'd in numbers ere the numbers came.*" And along with that there was of course a whole mysticism of sacred numbers, magic numbers, number symbolism. But I think what I was particularly interested in was how, in one line of the Jewish mystical tradition, letters & numbers converged, because the same symbols (the letters of the alphabet) were used for both. They were both the building blocks of the universe (a kind of mystical algebra) & a means for showing associations between words and phrases and utterances whose letters/numbers added up to the same sum. These associations then were something to consider: to accept, reject, or simply meditate on. And I was really surprised to see how far they had taken it –& interested in my own way in how that related to what seemed to me to be similar experiments in contemporary poetry, as in the work, notably, of artist-poets like Kurt Schwitters.

Q: Also we can observe that you speak about a movement that goes from myth through history to language and poetics per se and that your work by analogy with contemporary forms of poetry and art.

A: Well, I found that early in the twentieth-century there were a number of very interesting painters who were simultaneously writing poetry. That itself was of considerable interest. Schwitters for me may be the outstanding of them, and Hans Arp the most accomplished. There's also very interesting poetry by Paul Klee, theatrical experimentation by Kandinsky, and a lot of back & forth movement in general between the poets & the painters. I've always found it very curious how many poets have secret ambitions to be painters or painters to make poetry or to recognize an essential poetics in their approach to what they do as artists. So at certain points there has been a kind of unifying concept –of *art* as something bringing all these forms, approaches, mediums together. There is that which we have in common & that lets us learn about poetry from these artists' practice, not just with words as such but with colors, shapes, & visual forms. Some people are turned off by the big unifying movements of the early twentieth-century but I find a lot of kinship with them all along the line. Again, it was very interesting to me how much of the past began to open up & change through what I look to be an intense concern with how things were being done in the present –how much of the past in fact had opened up already for those predecessors. I think that if you work intensely in the present, it allows, even compels, an intense reconsideration of the past. Where the present idea of the poem changes sufficiently, then looking backwards at things that have been passed over, dismissed as not being poetry, shows them clearly as poetry, as very interesting, germinal poetry from which we can then learn in our attempts to create something like it in the present. The most obvious example, or the one at least to which I'm always referring, is the sound poem, the experiments by twentieth-century European & American poets to create a poetry without words. With that in mind it was possible to look back at the past –or to look at cultures very different from ours in the present– & to find in them songs, chants, structures that resembled language works but had no recognizable words in them. In other words, a poetry without words had existed, traditionally, in different times & places: magic formulas from the old Greeks & Hebrews, from Russian peasant cultures & many others, throughout the Indian Americas, & so on. Not simply a modernist invention, then, a Dadaist yoke, but a part of a common human inheritance. I don't know if that's the best or only way to view the past, but the impulse is there & very strong: to get past innovation for its own sake, or to let it link us to our origins as human beings *everywhere*.

Q: Is this related to the ambitious approaches you have been involved in –*deep image, ethnopoetics, total translation, poetics of performance*? Eshleman himself says that to read poets such as Olson, Duncan, McLow, Spicer, or you is more climbing a mountain than going to church.

A: I think what Eshleman is driving at is something I would subscribe to. The ambition of poetry in all of these cases is to go beyond literature, to go beyond what is narrowly described as poetry, to see it as part of a common mental & imaginal, even physical activity. The way the world –the mental, intellectual world– was divided up into units, compartments of academic studies –philosophy, history, art, & poetry, & so on– had a way a way of narrowing all those (call them) projects. And I think that at a certain point the effects on the making of poetry were disastrous. Poetry became too restricted in its possibilities. With predecessors like Blake & Whitman I find that it already begins to break open, to allow the poem to become involved with that whole range of human activities that the ambition you were speaking about clearly implies. I don't know if that creates a necessarily more difficult poetry in the process or that Eshleman has that in mind with the image of climbing the mountain. I think he means too that when you go into a church you have a fixed notion of what you're going to find, because this activity & ritual are so prescribed that everything that happens there is pretty much expected. By contrast the adventure of the mountain is that it takes one into new & possibly enchanted territory: wild & without borders.

So it's part of what we carry over from Romanticism: poetry as an act of discovery rather than a reiteration of what was always known to our *common* sense. Probably my own poetry, if it's what Eshleman says it is, seems to be more difficult than the poetry which simply explores immediate experience, although some very good things have come out of that too, so that it functions even now as a basis for most of our poetics. It hasn't been my practice to deny the poetry of the immediate or the experiential, but I'm not satisfied to let it go at that. I would try in my own way to open to those other possibilities –to question what we get both from experience & from tradition.

Q: In this sense are you interested in the reader in some way?

A: I think of myself as trying to be generous toward those who are reading my poetry or listening to it. I remember, when I was first working on **Technicians of the Sacred**, Louis Zukofsky questioned me about the large number of explanations I was putting into the book: those commentaries & so on that come in at the end. He said, *"Maybe it's not necessary to explain that much,"* but I've always had an impulse to explain. I have a reluctance, like Zukofsky & others, to put the explanation right in the poem, to crowd the poem itself with explanations. But then it seems to me, because I do want that interplay with the reader, that there must be other ways of allowing the reader an entry into areas of the poem, to points of reference that seem perfectly clear to me but may not be clear to them. What Dada is, what hasidism is: all simple surface matters. So when I did, say, a book like **That Dada Strain**, I tried with a short introduction to provide just a little bit of context, although I knew that for some, maybe most of my readers it was probably unnecessary . And I tried to pitch it not so much as explanation but as statement, letting some context come through in the course of it. A poet like Olson would invest a lot of time in talking between poems, so that finally a poet like David Antin can come along & make the talk itself into a kind of poem. And then a lot of the poets who most interest me have written a great deal *about* their poetry, their ideas of poetry at large, & the poetics that emerge from that kind of situation are the ones that I find of greatest value. Those make up the basic poetics that I read; the poetics of Pound, Breton, or Lorca, people who have written about it from the point of view of the practitioners. But about any particular poem what might be said about it or around it is what might otherwise be known if we still had a shared mythology, those things that might be held in common by a culture with a single body of tradition. Such a poem can be condensed, compact, because it caries all that knowledge that doesn't have to be expressed directly. As someone from one of those old cultures says (I'm paraphrasing from **Technicians**): *"The poem says so little because we know so much."* A lot of contemporary poetry carries that idea along as a kind of fiction –as if we really knew these things together.

Q: Which are the main theoretical lines behind ethnopoetics? What has been the role of the academy in its acceptance?

A: I saw it [ethnopoetics] as one of the working assumptions about the nature of poetry shared by a great number of contemporary poets. Although very little of the poetry in question had been gathered together in any systematic way by poets & artists as such, I'm sure there were aspects of ethnopoetics in the American line of Pound & Williams, in the

European surrealist line, in cubist & expressionist concerns with African poetry & ritual art: in short, a lot of predecessors for that work. Ethnopoetics was the term I made up & used to talk about those interests, particularly as related to tribal cultures that preceded the nation state or continued to exist outside it or at times within it, and in which the dominant form of communication was oral rather than literate. I suppose someone else might have a larger or narrower definition or framework for an ethnopoetics, but the term anyway was the one I chose for speaking about poetry over an expanded range of cultures, & I've continued to use it to the present. I don't otherwise know to what degree the word as such has come into any common usage. I suppose –as with other terms I've coined, like *deep image* & so on– that it ultimately creates as much confusion as clarity, but it remains for me a quick way of referring to that particular range of interests. The history of ethnopoetics in the academy is that it has been taken over by some people who, from a basically academic or scholarly perspective, are studying things like American Indian poetry and literature. The connection that I was trying to make –between ethnopoetics & the experimental poetry of the contemporary avant-garde– has largely been disregarded there. Even more radical academic movements like deconstructionism don't seem to have a corresponding interest in that sort of radical poetic practice –not even, say, in the work of the "language poets," who because of their own absorption of deconstructionist theory might be thought to have a special appeal to deconstructionist critics. But those critics, with some notable exceptions, seem to deal largely with conventional texts (if they deal with texts at all) & have turned largely toward a consideration of fiction & prose & away from any real concern with poetry as such. And, although it's very difficult for me to judge it, I would assume that the attitude toward my own work follows along those same lines, at least that I'm not one of the poets most studied or worked on at universities. I think that ethnopoetics has, if anything, become a kind of subfield in anthropology, as in the work of people like Dennis Tedlock & Dell Hymes, & that there's been a still more limited approach to it in academic literary studies, applying standard literary methods to things like Indian poetry & storytelling. (All of that shows up most clearly in a couple of anthologies edited by Brian Swann for the University of California Press, which have very little overlap with what Diane [Rothenberg] & I were doing, say, in **Symposium of the Whole**.) Ethnopoetics has also sometimes been confounded with the current interest in *ethnic* poetry to which it has some obvious relationship, although (I have to emphasize) it is clearly not the same thing. I don't think the academy, then, has any fundamental interest in most of these areas –certainly not the ethnopoetic & experimental, which don't have a constituency to bring some pressure on it.

Q: Can we speak about myth? Your poetic vision mixes different myths from various cultures, such as American Indian and Jewish. How is your approach & assimilation in relation to them?

A: Well, for me that's partly an experiential question. The Jewish mythology is something that I've been carrying around since childhood but that has opened & expanded for me over the past twenty, maybe twenty-five years. I was slow to come to it as a resource for my own work, but once I was into it, it began to shape a good part of my poetry. I don't know how necessary it is to a superficial reading of much of that poetry, but there are myths [mythic images] that very much prey on my mind & from there get into the work. I don't know if I would talk of them as *speaking* to me, as Duncan somewhere does [?], but I would be willing to say that as they speak to Duncan, so they speak to me. I can't comment on Duncan's experience of any of that, but in my own case, say, I might think of them appearing at times in dream & speaking to me in that sense, the idiomatic English sense of saying something speaks to me. They have meaning & resonance for as soon as I become aware of them. I experience a great sense of excitement & agitation about them until they finally find, make their way into the poetry. Even so I would hesitate to dramatize them as mythic beings who come to me directly & offer themselves to the poetry, & so on, & I would think that my experiences or Duncan's are in fact different in that way from the mythic & mystic apparitions that turn up for Blake. At least from my conversations with Duncan I don't think that he was really into *seeing* things in that way but again in the way that one can "*this myth 'really speaks to me.'* " The same to some extent with the Indian myths. There it really entered into my work at a point at which I had placed myself, experientially & for a number of years, in an Indian situation, until it was possible for me, to some degree, to use that in my own work. Not with the sense that I had somehow been transformed, had become an *Indian* in that process, but that something of that was now a part of the field of my own experience, that it could therefore speak to me, closely enough at least to make an entry to the poetry. I'm here talking about **A Seneca Journal**, say, or "Cokboy," rather than the anthologies, but I mean to say, even so, that I'm not seeing myself here as an Indian person but in another aspect of my own diaspora, the wanderings that take me into this or that place. Alternatively I suppose that I could deny the experience: I could pretend that I hadn't seen or been there, as if to satisfy those who might suppose that I *shouldn't* have been there in the first place, or I could remove it from the body of the poem. But obviously I've chosen there to let it all come in. Probably too there's a connection between the Jewish & the Indian myths –on some *deeper* level that ties myth into dream & other imaginal processes, while maintaining its reality in the world of *this* experience. Clearly in **A Big Jewish Book** or in "A Poem of Beavers," say, I'm exploring some of that common ground, even the curious way in which the Jewish tradition looks back to the period of the tribes/the tribal as a kind of golden age from which the people have emerged in movement toward their later disintegration/scattering. As another instance, the Jewish experience, while highly focused (as we know) on writing & the book, carries along a significant oral tradition [the "oral law" or "spoken torah"] that is reminiscent in its centrality of other tribal notions of the oral. Also there's a yearning, as with other displaced peoples, toward the place-of-origin, which is not only one of the complexities & difficulties of the current Israeli situation that has fostered for centuries the idea of displacement from that homeland which is at the same time the center of the earth, the center of the universe. And that has also got a very American Indian sense to it (& a chilling relation, let me add, to the Palestinian situation, as it now unfolds itself). I think of Jews & Indians alike as survivors –at least that with Indian poetry, as far as I've written about it, I've always tried to put a stress on survival or to not lose sight of the fact that while many Indian groups have experienced defeats & even genocide, others have survived & continue to survive into the present. I've tried to avoid the pathetic view of the Indian as the person who simply disappears, the person in the process of disappearing. That isn't to deny at the same time that some of these situations are culturally critical or desperate, that many of the Indian cultures are in a continuing state of crisis in which there's no absolute guarantee of their survival.

Some people have ben making those analogies between Jews & Indians for a long time, and some of them in retrospect now seem absurd or comical. The nineteenth century was filled with theories that tied Indians to the lost tribes of Israel, & certain aspects of American Mormonism, say, have carried that along. Many Indians I've known –older ones without a doubt– have had a kind of belief in some sort of relationship between Jews & Indians. Lame Deer I think it was made in interesting comment on Moses as a kind of Indian figure in the desert, the wilderness, listening like a shaman to the voices in the desert. But, again, you can do that kind of comparison between many different cultures, & I don't know if the Jewish & Indian comparison is any more or less valid than the others. It sounds funny, however, because of the other preconceptions about Jews & Indians that get in the way of it. For me at one point, anyway, I wanted both the reality & the absurdity of just that kind of juxtaposition, that quirky mix of myths & cultures. And the three *myths* I brought together, if you want to use that word, were those of the Jews, the Indians & the Dadaists.

Q: *Poland/1931* is a good example of the influence of myths in your literary experience. And it's very curious how the recurrence of some parts [titles? key words?] such as "Testimony," "Ancestral Scenes," "Polish Anecdotes," and even the graphics contribute to the myth/history depicted in the book.

A: Yeah, I think those are ways in which I can name certain kinds of experience in the writing that are recurrent for me. Certain poems, say, are presented as essentially small, anecdotal pieces, telling a little story or giving a rapid picture. The *histories*, which make up another category, are simple collages from fragments of prose material that I had been previously collecting as a file of details for inserting in the poems as such. (That is to say, the *histories* were larger chunks left over from the note-taking that was a part of my research for **Poland/ 1931**.) Then there were some poems presented as *amulets* in the book that came directly out of a magical tradition (or were made to look so) by translation or transcription. A number of my own poems look like they were influenced by that kind of poem-making as it shows up in kabbala or kabbala-related mysticism, & the *amulets*, in relation to that, are like markers to indicate that this kind of work isn't one of a kind but that it emerges in traditions outside of literary poetry. I think that all of that gives me a sense of shaping a book –something more comprehensive than the individual poems as such; that it lets me juxtapose the poems in the book in some sort of relationship to one another. It's in the nature of assemblage as it works itself out both in the book as a whole & in the separate sections. In that way the "testimonies" come together to form "a book of testimonies," the scattered descriptive bits & anecdotes come together to form a "book of histories," & so on. But the "histories" aren't confined to the "book" so named, but turn up again within the other sections, & that kind of recurrence, I think, adds to the sense of unity, of the book as a whole: a total work. My tendency has been to build up books in segments. In **Poland/1931**, for example, I'm bringing together a number of connected series that first appeared as separate smaller books or editions: **A Book of Testimony** that Tree Books published or **Esther K. Comes to America** that was first published by Unicorn Books. It's been my way of working or publishing for a long time now.

Q: You also seem interested in the role of the unconscious in the poem. What role does that concept play or what form does it take in the poetic process?

A: I think I spoke in terms of the unconscious during the "deep image" period, in the work I was doing in the fifties & early sixties. What it offered me then was a release from the dangers of overthinking a poem in the act of composition, & in that sense it was, I think, an instrument of liberation. Now I'm not sure if... I can never be sure of what's involved in any given poet's view of the unconscious. It first came into prominence with the French surrealists, the stress they put on automatic writing, which they defined in Freudian terms as the unmediated entry of unconscious thought processes into conscious, at least written form. But what emerged from all that had a serious resemblance to a kind of poetry that has been developed in Europe by poets up to & including the symbolists, and I came to wonder: if you got somebody else to write in that spontaneous fast way, someone without their *literary* background, mightn't the result be something very different? These after all are poets who are steeped in Baudelaire, Lautreamont, Rimbaud, Reverdy, & so on, by the time they come into their own experiments. And then they find that by dropping what feels to them like conscious intervention, by seeming to write automatically & unconsciously, so to speak, they create a written work that has striking resemblances to what seems like *poetry* to them. But there's already, I think, an idea of poetry that underlies that, so that what emerges from the process is conditioned in fact by the tradition that they're coming out of. There's more to it than that, but to put it in the most positive terms I can, I think that the encouragement toward writing without overthinking the process of the writing can at times be of the greatest use for any poet, that it can make all the difference at critical moments in the development of one's work: a recognition that a poem can be destroyed by too much as well by too little thinking. So I see it in that sense as part of a tradition that moves us into areas of spontaneity and improvisation in writing that remain important, whether or not you cast them in terms of the unconscious. It's of a piece, you know, with Tzara's declaration that "thought is made in the mouth," & so on. Don't labor the thought, in other words, but at a certain point, break down the barriers of premeditated thought to let something spontaneous, even surprising, rise up in the process of composition. That the mind —whether unconscious or not— is the reservoir of certain kinds of images, of mythic processes, is another very interesting and useful proposition, though I don't know if automatic writing is necessarily the key to that or if the usefulness of automatic writing is limited to the release of only those energies or possibilities. And if ideas of the unconscious are sometimes liberating, at other times I think they may involve a certain kind of self-delusion. You know: I've done this in a spontaneous, automatic way; therefore it must be good because I've gone about it in this good way... Chance operations, which the surrealists and the dadas were also concerned with, may curiously lead us in a similar direction.

Q: Clayton Eshleman recalls that Kenneth Rexroth once described you as "a swinging orgy of Martin Buber, Marcel Duchamp, Gertrude Stein, and Sitting Bull." Do you recognize this "definition"?

A: Well, that's one of the nicest things anybody ever said about me. I've always liked the combination, though I suppose what he's really pointing to there is the three-fold mythology

I was working out of: Jewish, Indian, experimental. Maybe a few others could be added.

Q: Your *New Selected Poems* has recently been published by New Directions. How does this make you feel, and what kind of poetic work will you be involved in form now on?

A: The "new" selected poems, as I say about them in a kind of pre-face to the book, are an attempt to show the continuity in the work since the earlier selected poems, **Poems for the Game of Silence**, which came out over fifteen years ago. My sense is that the poetry took a new turn with **Poland/1931**, that it continued with **A Seneca Journal** and **That Dada Strain**, and that it's still renewing itself in a very recent work that some people have been referring to as the new Poland poems & that New Directions will be publishing next year. I've also been continuing with experimental work using traditional Jewish numerological processes [*gematria*] of the kind we were speaking about before. **Poland/1931** was recently presented as a theatrical piece by the Living Theater, & I performed myself in a theatrical version of **That Dada Strain** in San Diego & then again in New York State. I continue to be interested in advancing the performance work, mostly in association with musicians, although it now seems possible to do it with theater people also. I've been doing a big translation work from Lorca, & I also want to do some serious translating from certain twentieth-century European poets like Kurt Schwitters, who still haven't come into English & so are largely disregarded here. But my overwhelming ambition, which I may or may not realize because it's such a big work, is to do a huge book of twentieth-century experimental poetry on something like a global scale. And that of course is not only an artistically work to pull of, but an economically difficult one as well. So I'll either do it in the next few years or else I'll assemble & publish whatever notes I make about it, & I'll let it go at that.

[NOTE. Since this interview was made, Jerome Rothenberg has completed the selected poetry of Kurt Schwitters (to be published by Temple University Press) & has been commissioned by the University of California Press to prepare a two-volume anthology of the twentieth-century avant-garde. Both books are being written and assembled in collaboration with Pierre Joris. The Lorca translations (of Lorca's **Suites**) are being published by Farrar Straus Giroux and **The Gametria** by Sun & Moon Press. What were referred to as the "new Poland poems" were published by New Directions under the title, **Khurbn & Other Poems**, in 1989.]

LESLIE SCALAPINO

Photo by Manuel Brito

Leslie Scalapino answered my questionnaire essaying about her main concerns. In fact, she suggests reading her "answers" as a complement to "What/Person: From an Exchange", an article she has co-authored with Ron Silliman in **Poetics Journal**, 9. My questions were centered around the psychological movement observed in her poetry, especially that produced by the narrative mode and poetic discourse as found in a given text, whether people are seen from an allegorical perspective in her poetry, issues raised from her conception about history and reality and, finally, about her interest in the visual arts because of her references to Picasso and Cindy Sherman. Even in her task as editor of the **O** anthologies, she selects poets who adopt a theory that goes beyond any literalness. Her poetry also shows communications on sex, social hierarchies, common and immediate places of our daily experience such as train stations, buses, restaurants, and so on. She was born in California in 1947 and graduated from the University of California at Berkeley. Her poetic production comprises such books as **O & Other Poems** (1976), **The Woman Who Could Read the Minds of Dogs** (1976), **Instead of an Animal** (1977), **This Eating and Walking at the Same Time Is Associated Alright** (1979), **Considering How Exaggerated Music Is** (1982), **That They Were at the Beach** (1985), **Way** (1988.)

As a fiction writer she has published **The Return of Painting, The Pearl, & Onion. A Trilogy** (1991) and she included essays and plays in **How Phenomena Appear To Unfold** (1990.) Along with her literary activity she has also been involved in editorship: **Foot** and O Books.

Q: *O and Other Poems* is dedicated to Virginia Woolf, to which degree can she be considered as a definite influence in your literary work?

A: I was reading Woolf (and Proust among many others) when I first began to write. I was influenced by Woolf's way of constructing a sentence: as sometimes paragraph-length with separate phrases which had *equal* significance (a *non-hierarchical* form of a sentence) held at the same time and apprehending many factors or perspectives in one moment of perception. (That is a very early influence.)

Q: Your essays seem to insist in the multi-perspective apprehension of reality, in this sense how do you interpret the poetic function?

A: A multi-perspective apprehension of reality is I believe apprehension or intrinsic to awareness per se; which I see as the poetic function. Any *doctrinal* orientation is distortion by definition constituting an interpretation; and thus since all perception is doctrinal or ideological in that sense, the *subject* of my writing is perception or perspective itself.

Q: You don' want the reader be restricted as an outsider but as a participant of the plot and form of the work, are you giving special emphasis to the "natural" reading?

A: You mention the notion of a "natural" reading which seeks to have the reader identify with the experience of the text, as different from a reading which is critically removed and aware of itself: I answered that my writing is constructing both of these experiences at the same time. So that the reader is aware of constructing his or her own perception or reality; which is not different from participating in it. Any view of *objectivity* as removed from and ahead of *experience* defining it, is per se a hierarchical imposition. (A conception of objectivity is implied in the description of being critically observant, an objective witness, as opposed to identifying with the object of observation. Ascendance of rationality as observational faculty is cultural fabrication.) The intention of my writing is to be aware of itself as cultural fabrication at the same time as revealing of being itself/oneself.

I recently had an exchange with Ron Silliman on this subject which will be published in the up-coming issue of **Poetics Journal**. My essential point in the exchange was that he was proposing such a notion of critical removal which is being distinguished from *identification* (that is, from *empathy*, which is held in our social scheme to be less credible as not being on a rational ground; we were debating writing related to matters of gender and race.) My point to him was that while he was proposing such a critical stance as a critique of the unified subject, such a view itself constitutes a unified subject.

Q: A combination of prose and verse is characteristic in some of your books, is this an epihenomenal structure or is it an intrinsic fact in your work?

A: This combination of prose and verse is an intrinsic factor of my poetic work in that it is a form in which all parts of a work are commentary on other parts. It is an observation of phenomena and mind play as the writing's sound, shape, and structure. The prose and verse at times echo sounds and shapes of each other (but differently) and at times diverge.

Q: In *Considering How Exaggerated Music Is* there's a psychological movement between the more narrative discourse which is inside the parentheses and poetic tone outside of them, how do you perceive that process?

A: In **Considering How Exaggerated Music Is**, the discourse inside and outside parentheses similarly comment on the discourse already occurring in the work at any point, and introduce new elements. It is a form of counterpoint. Thus the reference to exteriorized *social* places such as restaurants, train stations, buses and buildings (or humans as chameleon or semiotic figures) is the introduction of potentially endless new phenomena and the recognition that one cannot separate self from the *conception* of the social. This flattening and examination of mind phenomena is observation of conceptualizing; it is not allegorical. Its basis is the effort to apprehend the root of conceptualizing.

Q: *That They Were at the Beach* is a collection of poems and prose gathered in four sequences and you defined it as an "aeolotropic series", what do you mean by that?

A: The term "aeolotropic series" in this book refers to the fact that observation/interpretation of the reality of phenomena changes depending on the (locational, philosophical, cultural) perspective and (at the) time of observation. This process literally makes reality. No events occur in history or reality in the sense that they are only remembered later; they do not exist, and never did, the way they are remembered; yet are only that which is remembered by the individual as no one else remembers them in that way; if they are only remembered, they have no existence (in the present or past);' vast tracks of memory are not *notices* leaving only certain *chosen* elements which by such are distorted; *history* is only political and phenomenological distortion.

Thus (the condition of reality is that) any reader/writer is virtually in a sea of phenomena which can only be *interpreted* continually and individually. There is no valid hierarchical (philosophical or social) interpretation. My poetic structure and discourse seeks to understand that one exists in that condition, and to achieve clarity within it. (The best articulation of my poetics published thus far is I think **Way**.)

Q: Sex and genre are another subjects in your poems in your poems and essays, do you share a particular definition about feminism?

A: Defined simply, feminism is the rejection of the convention of male dominance in conceptual or institutional forms. It occurs only as experience, not as doctrine. We live the experiences of those conventions whether we want to or not. *Feminism* occurs in individual apprehensions in the poetic work, never in doctrine by its very nature already appropriated: as convention. The process of conventionalizing appropriates language and descriptions of experience to effectively negate and neutralize these. Academic conceptualization itself appropriates feminist theory and defines us in jargon; one counters this by refusing to use that language or conceive in terms of that discourse. That is, which includes the discourse of feminism itself.

Q: *O One. An Anthology* comes to be determined by the transgression of genres, as you say "between forms of poetic and critical discourse," how did you conceive it?

A: I did not have a conclusion but rather was interested to see how different writers were using forms transgressive of boundaries of poetic and critical discourse. My own use of this as I say has to do with breaking down the dualism between the conception of experience and conceptualization itself. For example, the piece of mine in the anthology is a play titled *Leg*; its conception as a play is multiple individual views which are a discourse or conversation and a poem, and are therefore *acts* as well as conceptions.

Q: Picasso and Cindy Sherman have been taken by you as motifs for developing your poetic ideas, are the visual arts so relevant and pertinent in your theoretical ideas?

A: I have been continually influenced by much visual art, in response to your question. My work is *visual* in the sense of creating a surface which appears to be objectively seen —and thus to raise the question of what that is; that which is *seen simply*, as if this were possible, becomes the ground of the examination of perception. Much as Cindy Sherman uses a multitude of disguised figures (who are herself); or Vermeer uses light.

The work to be published by North Point next June, **The Return of Painting The Pearl, and Orion/ A Trilogy**, is engaged with such matters of perception using vision as a strategy. Two works of the trilogy, **The Pearl** and **Orion**, use the form (as language only, not pictures) of the comic book in which each sentence or phrase is a frame in which there might be commentary observing the text or might be rendition of an action such as running. The text which has to do with one's construction of context and of the image, is sometimes prose, sometimes poems or indistinguishable as when the *paragraphs* of prose are only one line. Fiction, account, and commentary as the ground of examination of phenomena are flattened and ostensibly indistinguishable. There is the recognition that everything is fictionalizing. The form of this work apparently and as an action places the reader in the particular frame or place in time as it goes along, *objectively*, not ahead or behind; while observing oneself separating from what is occurring there. The writing is thus a form to see its own faculty and to see what one is.

RON SILLIMAN

Photo by Manuel Brito

To talk to Ron Silliman is to be conscious that we have to be ready to follow his energetic speech. His character is widely open and expressive but his cordiality is transformed in complex suggestion and rigorous thought when speaking about poetry. Silliman resists any poetic label. My own opinion is that his poetry raises ontological hypotheses of the individual within a social context where the events by themselves are not clarified. Doing so, he tries to immerse the reader in questions and discussions bringing forward subjective positions and social components that produce converging effects. It was a unique experience to meet Ron Silliman as a person and enjoy a poetry which is always risking honest and provocative compromises with life itself. Silliman was born in Pasco (WA) in 1946. He attended San Francisco State University and the University of California at Berkeley and I have to admit that it is almost impossible to review all the literary activities he has been involved in these last years. As a poet he has published **Crow** (1971), **Mohawk** (1973), **Nox** (1974), **Ketjak** (1978), **Sitting Up, Standing, Taking Steps** (1978), **Tjanting** (1981), **Bart** (1982), **The Age of Huts** (1986), **Toner** (1992), and in collaboration **Legend** (1980). He has also written six books of poetry more that make up a sort of epic series that follows and matches those of the greatest American poets and that is composed until now by **ABC** (1983), **Paradise** (1985), **Lit** (1987), **What** (1988), **Manifest** (1990), and **Demo to Ink** (1992). He has also co-authored **Leningrad** (1991) and published numerous poetic essays in many journals. His most decisive book of essays is **The New Sentence** (1987) that along with his editing of the anthology, **In the American Tree** (1986) have made him a key figure of the recent American poetry.

Q: Many critics have analyzed your work emphasizing the relationship between language and political items, but I consider that there are also ulterior motives, as we can observe in *Sunset Debris*, which require transcendental solutions by the reader.

A: There is no innocent writing. I take it that there are, at the very least, two levels of motivation along both the political and personal axes of any given act of writing –the level we know and another of which we are not (yet) aware. So, at the instant the pen first touches paper, we find no less than four orders of motivation present. On an entirely different plane, each act can also enter into any number of discourses, working with or against any variety of conventions, and setting them off into combination with one another. There is no upper limit.

This is why a one-word poem, such as Aram Saroyan's **blod**, can reverberate with an extraordinary density. The poem is mute about the stance it takes toward its own allusion to that charged noun *blood* and this silence can only be read as ambivalence. If we are aware of the person in the poem, of the author as context –and this of course will vary greatly with each reader– then we might be apt to read irony on the surface and an almost purifying rage beneath. Would we read this differently if somebody told us this were a poem "about" the Spanish Civil War, "about" HIV, or "about" pregnancy? Or if we discover that this text was created during the same historic period when visual artists like Claes

Oldenburg were constructing deformed commonplace objects, soft carrots and gigantic clothespins? The possibilities are infinite, even with a single word. What is not possible, it seems to me, is the reduction of the work to any single stabilized meaning. Meaning is no more stable than identity is continuous –such concepts are at best convenient myths that enable us to objectify our world so as to negotiate and manipulate it with a little less terror and wonder.

Those who have written about my poetry and its relation to politics have done so, I believe, from some sense that this aspect of my writing differed from that of my precursors. The underlying presumption is, or was, that the American avant-garde tradition lacked the political dimension that was so characteristic of European avant-gardes. But that was never true. The Objectivists were closely allied with one mode of Marxism. The San Francisco Renaissance had its origins in the concentration camps for war resisters during World War 2. Even during the McCarthy period of the 1950s, virtually all of the "New Americans" demonstrated politics in their writing. One can read Burroughs, for example, as an extended meditation on the relation between the state and the body. Kerouac's writing is profoundly aware of class. So, for that matter, is the work of Frank O'Hara, perhaps the first poet to sense (and certainly the first to articulate) the psychic gap that grows up around life in an office –that we do not identify with who we become on the job. But because the announced politics of a generation was articulated (even by many of the poets themselves, the notable exception being Amiri Baraka) as individualism –what Olson, that Democratic party activist, characterized as the Figure of Outward– it is easy to miss the deeper, more serious politics beneath.

A second critical approach has been an assertion that "political poetry" previously focused on localized topics –Oppen or even the surrealists might be the example posed– while my generation, by shifting attention constantly, even on a phrase-by-phrase, sentence-by-sentence basis, have proposed a more global politics in which the full range of everyday life is understood as always already fully politicized. But how does this differ from Zukofsky's **A** or Allen Ginsberg's **Wichita Vortex Sutra**? The difference, I suspect, lies not so much in those texts as in how they were read and contextualized.

The problem of transcendence is that it too is a political category. There is, in this sense, no outside. It is just that constraint, that as humans in a limited universe we must ultimately rely upon our own devices and those of the biosphere, which creates this phenomenon of excess that underlies the unpredictability of change. Totality is "achieved" in any only by ignoring the nagging little details at the margin. Yet those are what accumulate, floating free until they arrive at a critical mass that so often comes as a surprise.

Q: Sometimes you use an abstract language which makes us think there's some possibility of deciphering the alphabet of our culture, that is, is the systematization another way of finding a different system?

A: When I began writing **Ketjak** in 1974, I wanted a mechanism that would force me to break away from traditional prose structures which tend to equate narrative (which I define as the unfolding of meaning in time) with plot. Since I intended to utilize sentences that were, by themselves, syntactic, representational, and not inherently "unusual," I found that a system which "arbitrarily" determined the order of sentences provided the freedom I sought. Seventeen years later, it's hard to remember just how difficult it seemed to me at the time to simply compose a sentence that didn't necessarily depend on its predecessor for context in a purely pictorial or argumentative manner. If anything, the method now freed context up to become far more forceful, because it no longer depended upon a reductivist signified.

The three works that round out the first stage of my project –the texts gathered under the title **The Age of Huts**– all reflect that original struggle. **Sunset Debris** exploits parallel syntax as its alternative, and a close reading will reveal that there's actually not that much movement between questions. **The Chinese Notebook** isn't systematic in the slightest, and each paragraph can be read as a distinct work. 2197 used the most complicated –and to my mind least successful– system I've employed in its attempt to break sentences down internally.

The next stage of my project, **Tjanting**, was in some ways as surprising to me as **Ketjak** had been, but for exactly opposite reasons. When I started the work, I had not realized that there would come a moment in each paragraph when the repeated "intervening" sentences would run out before I had completed the number of sentences that the paragraph required. So I was forced to try writing "freely." I remember worrying at the time that those passages would collapse into something less interesting. Instead, what I learned was that I really had grown able to focus on the sentence itself, and that I no longer required "systems" as such to structure the work in some fashion other than plot or hierarchic exposition.

I read **Tjanting** as the second stage of my project, parallel (i.e., neither higher, nor lower) to the first. The next stage, parallel to these first two –and to my reading a balance to that earlier ensemble– is **The Alphabet**. A major question of **The Alphabet** is: if I do not require systems in order to generate forms whose purpose is to defeat linearity in reading, what then is the role

of form. After eleven years of working on this question, I am
still not certain that I am close to any answer. Indeed, it took
me over ten years just to recognize that this was one major
question of the project.

I should note that I do not read **The Alphabet** as a series of
poems. To me, a series requires that individual units or sections
take an equivalent form, such as John Berryman's **Dream Songs**.
Rather, I see **The Alphabet** as a poem composed of poems.
Similarly, this larger structure I've just mentioned, including
those two historically earlier stages, is itself to my mind a
single poem. What I am writing is one poem. That it may
composed of poems is a problem more for poetry than for me.
Overall, I have always thought of this project as **Ketjak**. So
The Alphabet is a part of **Ketjak**, just as the next paragraph
of the original **Ketjak** (specifically titled **Ketjak 11: Caravan
of Affect**), one of the sections (or poems) I working on at the
moment, turns out to be part of **The Alphabet**.

What I don't want to do is to make any claim for a metonymic
relation between my own working processes and the world at
large. That sort of hubris for the long poem, which I take as
central to its problematic dating back to Dante if not Homer,
and evident in a particularly caricatured form in the work of
Pound and Olson, is precisely the totalitarian moment in poetry
I seek to challenge.

It seems to me that the question I'm asking by taking this
approach is not just what is the relation of form to the poem,
and of poetry to form, but also what is the relation of poetry
to a life. My life. Writers who have asked this question in the
past –Robert Duncan, for example– have responded by exploiting
life's indeterminacy as a model for the poem. That seems to me
inadequate, although perhaps less so than the attempt to construct
the poem as a cathedral, such as Ronald Johnson's **Ark**. That

makes poetry a religion, a totality, a lie. Not unlike my position within the American left, attempting to discern a practical path between the totalitarian impulses of Leninism and the hopeless corporatism of social democrats, I am still searching out a third way in the poem.

Q: Some of the poets of past decades used specific references to the quotidian, but also to mythology, traditional items, etc. However most of the language poets seem not to be interested in historical allusions or classical references.

A: Immediately, Barrett Watten's use of historic reference in **Progress** comes to mind, as do the classic references that permeate the work of Bob Perelman, Tom Mandel, Steve Benson, and David Melnick. James Sherry's **Our Nuclear Heritage** is unquestionably a "poem containing history." Where the current generation differs from some of its predecessors, however, may be in the value presumed by the use of such reference. A poet such as Olson used history as a legitimating discourse for his verse. He used both history itself, which gave him something to write about, and the prestige of history as a practice. Often, I think, he used that prestige rather obnoxiously. Unfortunately, this is the only aspect of the strategy which comes through today in the writing of someone like Paul Metcalf.

Suggesting that your assertion here is inaccurate, however, really only touches on part of what I think you are getting at here. The substantive question, I believe, is not one of the use versus non-use of historical or classical discourse, but of the different use. I have always felt, for example, that Allen Ginsberg's **Wichita Vortex Sutra** was a far better model for the uses of history in a poem than those posed by Pound or Olson.

Q: In your poetry there is a mixture of visual and phonic images like "Green glass broken in the grass" along with statements like "one writes to discover who is doing the writing." Isn't there any kind of intentionality by the author upon the reader in this sense?

A: Of course. My writing seldom aims to focus on just one of the functions of language. More often it alternates between different kinds of sensation, such as sound or sight, and various degrees of argumentation, ranging from the metalinguistic to some high order abstraction like political theory. The movement between these domains seems as important as anything I might write within a particular sentence or line. I do believe that language is fundamentally sensuous, and that one of its most vital aspects is just this richness of possibility. But I also believe that human consciousness and identity are not continuous. Who "I" am is constantly under reconstruction. My movement between sentences is the best approximation I've been able to come up with for that process of constant refocusing that we each do constantly in our lives.

Q: Behind the occasionality of the sentences or words like "thump," as you explained to your Old Left friend, isn't there a desire of communicability even though we answer "I don't understand?"

A: Communication, yes. Communicability I'm much less certain of. That term implies a reliance on the signified that must always be separate from communication as such.
What is communication? Think of Roman Jakobson's six functions of language, those elements which must always be present: signifier and signified, addresser and addressee, contact

and code. Jakobson actually uses the term context in place of signified, and in that sense it seems quite evident that "thumpa" presents a rich range of context. In the Robert Grenier poem from which this word is taken,

thumpa
thumpa
thumpa
thump

the term suggests American graphic conventions for the representation of non-linguistic sounds, including such diverse examples as the rhythm of a locomotive or the compulsive foot-stomping of Disney's cartoon rabbit, Thumper, in the film **Bambi**. Thus, as is virtually always the case, nonsense is a particularly complex instance of sense itself, not its erasure or Other. Here, *thumpa* is a "non-word" that points to a surprisingly large body of other "non-words," all of which exploit the social category of the non-word as an aspect of their own agency. The onomatopoetic loses its force if we don't acknowledge its special condition and thus becomes "only" a word.

Communication seldom enough communicates only or even primarily the signified in the ordinary uses of language in everyday life, and almost never does so in literature. One function for literature, in fact, is to heighten our awareness to what else is present within any linguistic act. One aspect of this particular instance is code, which for English includes that special category of words that deny their own legitimacy as language. Even more the powerfully active, I believe, is contact, that most mysterious of all of Jakobson's categories, the recognition and acknowledgement of the presence of an Other. By picking a term that denies its own linguistic status, and which (through precisely its social background in popular cinema and literature) hides both identity and agency, *thumpa* wishes to reduce its moment of poetry to the almost pure instant of recognition and acknowledgement. *Thumpa* asserts that presence alone constitutes communication.

Because Derrida, in particular, mounted such an effective assault on the prestige of presence in establishing the groundwork for a deconstructive practice, we have never had a real analysis of presence's political content and implications. This feels like an increasingly serious omission, because it has prevented us from fully confronting the meaning of both identity and agency, the two components of presence. Yet without such an analysis, many linguistic and symbolic acts remain mute and beyond our response. In the United States, this has enabled many people, including a few on the left, from recognizing that the yellow ribbon used as a symbol during the war in the Persian Gulf is no more than a soft, postmodern version of the swastika. Like the swastika, the ribbon has no meaning other than as a cipher for presence, the presence of militarized nationalism posed as a unified will. While presence has by no means only negative meanings (as its role at the heart of intimacy shows), this example should underscore why it is important that we confront the problem directly.

Q: Stephen Fredman appears three times on the back covers of your books with same sentence: "Silliman offers a grand example of the crisis in verse." Will stability come back to poetry?

A: That's not a question for poetry, but for society. There certainly is a community within the field of the poem that values this genre precisely for its premodern tradition. These anti-modern individuals are attracted to a poetics of visible order, preferably with a subtext for the poem related to class background and orientation. It's a distinctly bourgeois poetics and, not surprisingly, many of its practitioners and readers take the poetry of the United States to be a tributary of British literary tradition. While this community has been with us for a long time, it currently practices under the name of the New Formalism.

But this premodernism, it seems to me, is wildly out of touch with the real world. The world on which it was presupposed ceased to exist with the invention of the cotton gin and the evolution of industrial capital. Today we live on a planet where technological change transforms social and political relations in ways that not even Walter Benjamin could have foreseen. For example, we can see what the necessity of a militarized economy has meant to the Soviet Union, having to compete with the technologically superior United States. Without the technological drivers that have governed U.S. military ordinance since World War 2, the Soviet Union was forced to spend such a large portion of its gross national product that the Russian economy has simply collapsed. And we have very recently seen in Kuwait and Iraq how this same U.S. technological superiority has transformed classic military equations about the premises of force. If you can kill 100,000 people, as the so-called Coalition did, while losing less than 100 of your own soldiers –and without having to resort to nuclear weaponry to accomplish this mass-scale homicide– you have permanently changed what other nations must take into account before they embark on any actions you might oppose.

Technology is having very much the same impact domestically. It's role in the structure and life of corporations has made many of them as powerful as states. Indeed, both the European Community of 1992 and the recent attempts by the United States to remilitarize foreign relations (first by the R&D focus of star wars, and then much more successfully through the gradual escalation of U.S. interventions, beginning with Grenada, then Panama, and now Iraq) can be viewed as attempts to "rescue" the state from the technological advance of civil society. The collapse of states in Eastern Europe shows us that such attempts may only be postponements of an inevitable transition to a new society in which the state has withered while capitalism has indeed become all the more assertive.

I realize that what I'm writing can be read as a kind of technological determinism. That would be a mistake because technology itself is remarkably indeterminate and subject to social conflict. IBM has imposed an inferior model computer keyboard on the PC industry, with the function keys across the top rather than on the left where they're far more readily accessible to the fingers of the left hand, simply because IBM is the largest manufacturer of microcomputers. But the bottom line here is that stability in society necessarily relies upon underlying cyclical patterns like those which dominate agricultural, pre-industrial civilizations. We have not had this in centuries, and are not apt to have it again unless we inadvertantly bomb or ozone ourselves back to the stone age. To the degree that poetry will always be integral to the society which produces it (a far more complex relation than simple reflection), poetry itself can never again imagine itself to exist outside of time.

Q: There is an irony in your theoretical work where you speak about the subversion of classical roles, such as non-representation versus representation, non-function vs. function. Is it likely that this non-referential work will end as a representation?

A: Absolutely. In fact, non-representation always already is a mode of representation. Like chaos, which is not disorder at all but rather a specific mode of order, all language is referential, so that non-referentiality turns out to be a specific subset of reference, one where the usual extra-linguistic gestalt mechanisms that are applied to language have been temporarily cancelled or blocked. Generally, this is the case for other such categories as well.

To come back to Jakobson's six functions, what I above called signified (and which he calls context) is precisely what North Americans normally understand by the term reference. No doubt context is more accurate ultimately than signified, but the Saussurean-Lacanian pair (S/s) have become so widely known in the United States that it seems more practical to substitute signifier and signified for Jakobson's terms, message and context. The substitution also makes clear that Jakobson's six functions really are a triad of oppositions:

Addresser/Addressee

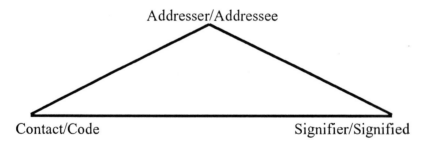

Contact/Code   Signifier/Signified

In practice, communication configures this triad so that one of pair of oppositions is highlighted. Simultaneously, one element of each pair is given greater weight. Non-referential writing places a very high value on the signifier with a corresponding negative value given to the signified. This is just another way of saying that the context for a word or sentence has been removed, so that the material letters or sounds are foregrounded. Once Clark Coolidge demonstrated how this could be done, in works such as **The Maintains**, where he arrives at have something very close to a strict non-referentiality, poets very quickly began to explore the more complex and less extreme gradations of this process.

For example, Peter Ganick's poetry foregrounds sound, the aural signifier. He's wonderful to listen to, but if you just see the poem on the page without sounding it yourself, you are apt to miss what is going on. That orality places a significant (tho secondary) weight on contact within the contact/code opposition and the least weight on the addresser/addressee opposition (tho again it assigns a weight, here on the addresser, the origin of the sound). All communication develops these oppositions into such little hierarchies, and Ganick offers only one mode of non-reference. A text that focuses on the signifier, but then on the code rather than the contact might be one of Charles Bernstein's typing pieces, which have an historic kinship to concrete verse. To simply call either type non-referential still leaves unsaid much about what goes on.

Q: It seems you like the idea of things left unfinished. Is this more truthful or simply responds to our contemporary age?

A: What is more true than our contemporary age itself? Or, as Stanley Fish and Fred Jameson call it these days, our post-contemporary age. After all, history, however indeterminate, has led to this.

Actually, each of the works I've written to date, from **Ketjak** through the seventeen completed sections of **The Alphabet** has had a clear moment of closure, even though those moments are often ironized in the text itself. Yet the larger poem that each is also a part of is quite obviously far from complete. I can't even begin to tell you what the next stage should look like, because I certainly don't know. An **Encyclopedia** seems possible, but problematic. Or I might switch altogether and write a series of detective or science fiction novels. Or I might utilize computer technology and do multi-media presentations or hypercard stacks. I don't think there's anything presently in the work to preclude (or, alternatively, preselect) any of those alternatives.

The underlying tension here is that closure requires social convention at its most brazen –endings are always arbitrary, so the entire trick, something that the realists learned (rather the hard way) over a century ago. Critics like Jameson, who fixate their definition of modernism on those works and artists who, having learned that closure is always a lie, continue to invent artificial methods for ending their texts, just as Joyce's **Ulysses** or the too-precious works of Eliot and Stevens, are unable to see how other writers, such as Dickinson, Stein, Whitman, or Zukofsky, who are far less interested in the problem of closure, more accurately reflect the conditions of a world in which the onrush of capitalist technological development has permanently thrown over the organicist closure of "natural" cycles. That understanding is what makes William Carlos Williams' **Spring & All** the defining poem of the first half of the 20th century, at least for me. I'm including the prose in that text in my definition of that work as a poem.

In my own writing, I prefer to focus such moments on the relation of form to convention, pointing out that convention always means an agreement between parties, writer and reader, that must rest on the arbitrary. If you can pose it effectively, you can expose the power relations which serve to enforce these agreements.

Q: Could graffitiing consonants and vowels in a sentence become as psychotic as smoking a cigar?

A: Smoking cigars is a form of willful suicide. Consonants and vowels are curiously phonic subdivisions of the alphabet around which historic rules for syllabification cluster. Vowels and consonants are themselves historic clusters of phonemes. Liquid consonants –*l*, *m*, *n*, and *r*– appear almost androgynous: they share qualities we associate with vowels. Unlike Hebrew, our writing presents no graphic indication of which letters are which. Yet we continue to believe in the essence of a vowel. As children, we recite and sing vowels over and over.

Q: Tautologies like 'what you read is what you read' celebrate non-intentionality, but at the same time they stimulate to us find out ulterior theoretical backgrounds.

A: I disagree that such statements celebrate non-intentionality. Rather, they acknowledge that intentionality is elsewhere in much (perhaps most) of the language we consume, especially through reading. Advertisers know that to "hear" a message is to have articulated it to yourself internally. In a talk that I gave recently –first in Tuscaloosa, Alabama, and later in Houston, Texas– I discussed some of the literary and political implications of signage:
The writing on the cafeteria wall is like much (possibly even most) of the written language Americans consume today in that it contains no tangible presence of a subject. Street signs, underwear labels, the narratives on our boxes of cereal, the questions our computers ask of us –all share this linguistic stance of anonymity. The tone of an absent-but-neutral subject is so common among newspaper headlines that a publication

which strays from the norm, such as the **Village Voice**, the **New York Post** or even the **National Enquirer** is immediately perceptible as distinct, with much personality. (The **Voice's** headlines, for example, make much use of puns, jokes, alliteration and allusion, while its roster of hot books, subtitled **Our Kind of Best-Sellers,** announces the presence of a subject by foregrounding the possessive.)

Not surprisingly, much (although not all[1]) of the anonymous and thoroughly commercial language of daily life is constructed around what Charles Bernstein calls the normative or plain style of grammar. This discourse of the social contract is writing in the purest Derridean sense –even in its most truncated forms, as on the cafeteria wall, it insinuates a universe of order, a hierarchy made to seem natural. Today, of course, this writing invades our speech as well. Communications technology, such as phone mail or those interactive systems that permit us to inquire about our bank balance from a touch-tone phone, extend this phenomenon beyond the written word.

Far from being incidental, the instrumental language of an absent subject has, in the past half century, created a pervasive tone. This constant, not-quite-subliminal static, like the irritating electronic hiss of a cheap tape deck, forms the ground against which we consume all "postcontemporary" experiences of discourse, spoken or written.

Q: Now three questions which are taken from your own work:

   a) What makes you think you have choices?

A: Certainly one's options in life are limited. I was fortunate to have been born a white male in the most affluent nation on earth. That I was born into the least affluent family in my community, that I was raised in a household with one psychiatrically disabled adult, that I was raised in a household with few books and no music, that my father was a brawler who ran off when I was an infant, and that my mother, my great-grandmother, and my great greatgrandmother all were single parents –all equally shaped my life. These are only a handful of a million such details.

The question is how does one respond? If intentionality is elsewhere, as I have just argued, any act of resistance must entail choice.

Politics is a process, not a project. It has no teleological meaning. If we understand this, then choices are precisely what we do have. They may be limited, and they may not all be good ones, but our own sense of self requires that we choose.

Subjectivity has two components: identity and agency. One cannot have one without the other. Agency implies choice.

b) If you know how to survive, do you know what you do?

A: To cite Ms. Stein, "What is the question?"

c) What did Bernstein say to make you ask so many questions?

A: If you are referring to **Sunset Debris**, it wasn't Charles at all who provoked that work. At that time, Kathy Acker was reinventing the novel for her own uses, publishing one chapter each month through small xeroxed editions. Her early works –**I Dreamt I Was a Nymphomaniac Imagining, The Childlike Life of the Black Tarantula** (that was actually her pen name during much of that period), and **The Adult Life of Toulouse Lautrec**– mixing pornography and plagiarism to arrive at autobiography, struck me then as the most courage acts of writing I had ever seen. Now that I am old enough to understand her writing as a continuous meditation on the implications of childhood sexual abuse, they seem even braver to me today.

In that context, it was impossible not to want to write a work that was thoroughly uncompromising. I have my own issues with the questions of power, quite apart from those I saw in Kathy's writing, and I had been working for several years at that point with prisoners, mostly in California. I wanted a work that was relentless in exposing the unequal power relations of the text. **Sunset Debris** was the result.

March 27, 1991

---

[1] Advertisements (especially lines and slogans) are the most noteworthy exception, driven by a need to foreground themselves against the constant recessive chatter of all this other language.

BARRETT WATTEN

Photo by Manuel Brito

If I have to apply to any poet the qualifying adjective of scientific or methodical, I'd select Barrett Watten as the poet who works most rigorously among stanzas with circular and convergent procedures. On few occasions have we the opportunity of seeing that a dramatic and apparently nonperceivable dialogue becomes an argument of silogisms by itself with further explorations. He considers poetry a questioning act, since he acknowledges that "each sentence admits the faults of individual words" and so it's not easy to overcome those conflicts so internal to ourselves and to verbal language expression. His intellectual poetry plays with the dictionary and the crossword; it can return us to the Russian formalists, Olson, Postmodernism, Surrealism, the literary community he is involved in, Coolidge, or Crane's poetics. It's a poetry that gives no rest to thought. Watten is another poet whose literary activities have covered a wide range of interests since 1972: poetry, poetic essays, art criticism, radio broadcasts, lectures, and workshops. Born in California in 1948, he attended Massachusetts Institute of Technology. He got an AB, Biochemistry, from the University of California at Berkeley and an MFA from the University of Iowa. Among his books of poems we have to mention **Radio Day in Soma City** (1972), **Opera Works** (1975), **Decay** (1977), **Plasma/Paralleles/"X"**

(1979), **1-10** (1980), **Complete Thought** (1982), **Progress** (1985), **Conduit** (1986), **Under Erasure** (1991). He has also written in collaboration **Leningrad** (1991) and a thoughtful book of essays, **Total Syntax** (1985). Being the editor of **This** (1971-1982), **Poetics Journal** (1981-) has helped to increase his relevance to contemporary American poetry.

Q: Would you describe the theoretical background of what another poet has called your "aesthetic program"?

A: My "aesthetic program," in brief, would be to extend the autonomous structure of the "aesthetic" into the temporal continuum of the "ideological." This is hardly radical, going back in English literature at least as far as Chaucer and Margery Kempe, and certainly not unique: today in the mail I received an image on a postcard from the Phyllis Kind Gallery in New York titled *America with Intersections and Walmarts*, by Roger Brown. I experienced this image as a temporal intervention in an ongoing dialogue in which cultural meanings ("America") are being constructed (on a stylized, coded map, each state contains its own geometrical mall); the artist's irony is to mimic the latest advance in schematic understanding, yielding an overview that at the same time cancels any pretentions. But clearly an exception would be implied if ongoing cultural projects, such as this one or my own, are being characterized as following a "program." "Program" implies method; methods are totalizing, therefore totalitarian; and if there is an "aesthetic program," I hear it being asked, does it include me?

That an "aesthetic program" would be thought to exclude "me" seems to go to the heart of what makes it seem frightening. In America, at least, this *me* comes along with an "aesthetic program" of its own, a "program that is no program" in which a versified practice of self-expression addresses the world

directly from the position of a reactive "me." That would be
the gist of the argument "we" (myself and five other writers)
made in our collaborative article "Aesthetic Tendency and the
Politics of Poetry" (**Social Text** 19/20). But it is perhaps too
simple to find "expressivist" poetry self-contradictory in
disavowing its own "aesthetic program." Recently I encountered
an interesting work by Diane Di Prima in the un-self-oriented
context of an AC Transit bus in Berkeley:

NUMBERS RACKET

when you take no for an answer
will you look any different
will you get pale
behind your glasses will you
go backward with that
funny step
will you straighten your jacket

I mean are you taking it.
now, taking no
for an answer

This is a very good poem for mass transit, the best of the genre
I have encountered. It is clear that it means to reproduce an
ideological effect: that moment Louis Althusser speaks of when
"ideology hails us," which Ron Silliman, in turn, has translated
as "Hey, you, get off of my Cloud!" Public identity is a
consequence of denial in this poem, and the poem's lower-case
vocalizing –imitating the suppressed voice of resentment that
goes along with such a "no"; "I mean are you taking it," such
a public person might ask him or herself –makes that effect an

immediate and everyday "now." But how does the poem intervene? By introjecting its own denial of the everyday man who shapes up to the denying norm, straightening his jacket and going pale behind his glasses, the poem says it could be otherwise: you could do what you want (presumably, win the sweepstakes and leave by next plane to Bermuda). The poem, and the poet's expressive voice behind it, is on the side of desire.

But is this how poetry on the busses really works? Another example, a poem by Michael Smith, equally vocalizes a response to the confines of negation: "i / shall not die / a natural death / but fighting" —is the alternative commute an instantaneous terrorism, a short-circuit out of the "system"? Both poems, in fact, seem to present themselves equally as objects of reflection, expressively true but ironically received, as much as direct communication. This effect would be increased by the numbers of times a given bus rider would encounter these particular messages —next to Army recruitment posters, ads for hemorrhoids and business colleges, AIDS-awareness campaigns. "Oh, there's that guy dying an unnatural death trying to fight the system for the eighty-ninth time," he or she may reflect. Here expression of a singular and untenable insight becomes a persistent redundancy, and whatever expressive intention exists would be lost as simply a reflective moment competing for attention with numerous other sales pitches.

Even so, the ratio here between private expression and public scale is significant —both for what it is as expression and for what it recursively inculcates in the subject. It is clear that freedom on the expressive side of these poems is equally matched by denial in their reception; this disparity is, exactly, their ideological effect. Social reality is a lie built upon the truth of *me*, and it will always defeat *me* —that's how I know what it is. This aligns perfectly with Slavoj Zizek's remark that "the idea of the possible *end* of ideology is an ideological idea *par excellence*." Thus Zizek finds in Althusser's critique of ideology "a radical ethical attitude which we might call the heroism of alienation." An "aesthetic program" stemming from this attitude would interest me very much; so in an acknowledgment of social negation based on the experience reproduced in Di Prima's bus poem, I wrote:

> The station maintains its output. White noise spreads from static generators built with that in mind.
>
> Severed heads fill in the gaps.
>
> An unending series of negatives is the signal for collapse. Block by block the power fails. Power poles spread out at equal intervals down the street.
>
> The train arrives from nowhere. Music follows the engine's path through space.
>
> The finished product comes to light. ("Paralleles")

The "finished product" here (at least this fragment of it) may be due more to "method" than to "expression," although one could say that, finally, the dizzying affect created by these simultaneous blanks, negations, and assertions is as expressive of a state of mind and as other-directed as Di Prima's address to the bus rider. The sequence here, however, does not necessarily follow in the same order as Di Prima's assumption, statement, and identification; rather a statement is being built from "integral components" of identification and is then given the rhetorical form of a synthetic argument. This argument, however, may have formal properties more like the total experience of signs encountered in social space on the bus than like any "single moment" that "expressivist" poetry would inculcate in its public. This kind of formal recombination, then, is where I begin in my "aesthetic program," but I don't consider that it is where I end –it is not just the vertiginous pleasure of running up and down the scale of these fragmented denials, nor the "finished product com[ing] to light," but a simultaneously more public and more psychological poetics that I want.

Q: I wonder if all the concepts and proper names listed in "Index to Introduction" can be considered as essential components in your poetic development?

A: I think of "Index of Introduction" not just as a set of references to artists and movements important to my work –like Russian Formalism, Art-Language, Roman Jakobson, Larry Eigner– but as a (perhaps ironic) comment on the process of learning. In a literal sense: this was the result of my first attempt at indexing the introduction to **Total Syntax**; clearly I hadn't got the principles of indexing right and was creating a great deal of redundancy by virtue of the categories I had set up. Neither the level of reference nor the subdivisions into various components of the argument worked; the list became repetitive and missed the point entirely. Subsequently I learned to index in another way; an index like this for the entire book would have been nothing but an impediment.

It is included as one section of "The Word" because it typifies excessive and redundant aspects of indexicality that, in other sections of the poem, characterize texts in general. While texts purport to be communicative, and to present systematically the material under their purview, they generate in their own materiality a displacement that seems to me to have comic value. If in "Conduit" "speech is the sound of what's missing in writing," here the sound of writing is a continuous verbal gag. That is what it invariably turns into when I read it out loud –its insufferable length and redundancy yields titters, then genuinely throaty haws. As such it seems to reverse the kind of anxiety present in the rest of my work, where no matter how humorously displacing a given textual moment may be, it evokes more a kind of participatory *ostranenie* (defamiliarization) than any immediately gratifying release of energy on the part of an audience.

In this sense "Index to Introduction" seems to put into practice, on advantageous terms, one of my most recurrent "performance anxiety" dreams. I am called upon to give a poetry reading, but on the way to the reading I have somehow forgotten my manuscripts and books. Never mind, I'll improvise, and proceed to do a stand-up improvisation reading names, addresses, and numbers out of the phone book. About a page or two into it I come to my senses; some version of this dream is I think very common among writers. It seems to me that one interest of Jackson Mac Low's "indexical" work –for instance, **Words n Ends from Ez**– is its acting out of a similar scenario. One might see an instance of "anxiety of influence" here in Mac Low's dismantling of the authority of the **Cantos**, and this connects to the list of names in my own index. Certainly, these names are important forebears, but perhaps it turns out (already has) that all such exemplars are systematically redundant.

Q: Voloshinov says that ideology is a matter of signs and is not related to consciousness. Can the dictionary, speech, the poem itself be completed without propositions elaborated by the sensibility of the subject?

A: By saying that ideology is material, Voloshinov means that is located in the space between subjects. I might say, "Blackbirds on a line sing a raucous tune and Russia is electrified," and it would sound like ideology in Voloshinov's sense. But for Voloshinov it is also the subject's organization and subordination of this material speech that gives evidence of its ideological effects (as having created an intersubjectivity). Here it seems that the material/psychological distinction is beginning to break down. I would allow it to break down all the way and say, with linguists like Charles Fillmore and George Lakoff, that the material sign is implicitly bound up with cognitive frames and categories. So as language, the privileged terms of a culture are psychologically as well as materially real. Further –thinking of psychoanalysis in the way that Lacan does when he recounts the anecdote of his conversation with a fisherman, "Do you see that sardine can floating in the water? Well, it doesn't see *you*! –there really can't be any separation between material signs and their psychological reality insofar as we speak of ideology. The repetition of material signs –for example, the American flag symbolizing "Victory"– is both created by and creates a psychological reality, in this case the auratic excess of national glory. I would be interested in an American flag in its complementary colors –for red, green; for white, black; for blue, orange– that, given its ubiquitous repetition, would have the opposite effect. Some of the statements in my poems I hope might work that way when experienced cumulatively.

What would such a notion of "complementary" meaning, that when experienced long enough would create its opposite, like repeating "money" 100,000 times a day to cure avarice, entail? Something like Wittgenstein's rabbit/duck, to be *seen as* differently in different environments of use? If Wittgenstein's figures achieve their effect by virtue of commitments exterior to any subject (that would be one way of thinking of a "language game"), there might be a tricky way that the materiality of signs returns, as a modernist paradigm, to have a specifically ideological role. "Exterior" contexts are constructed from "interior" identifications in the case of the rabbit/duck; so in a politically charged environment, the rabbit might be *seen as* a peace sign, and the duck its depoliticized complement. Such a materialization of "inner states" and a psychologization of "exterior" ideology coexist characteristically in modernism, and that is how I would read Voloshinov.

The question then would be, What kind of psychology goes along with this materialization? In Jerome McGann's salutary project of reading the romantic poets specifically to avoid their subjective unity (or the equivalence of psychological reality with ideological effects), the material fact of their texts is proposed as basis for a subsequent history. That history is its reception and "judgment" as being meaningful as much as it is its bibliographical trajectory, of course; and so one must still speak of specifically textual subjectivity effects. Take McGann's discussion of Pound's **Cantos**, for instance: while bracketing out subjective intention in Pound one might still be painfully aware of slippages of meaning caused by the redundancies of the text ("Out of all this beauty something must come") and a concomitant fetishization of further increments of "material" information, such as the Chinese characters laid into the text as virtual printers' dingbats. One visualizes the film version of Pound's relation to the material text: a crotchety old man literally hitting the **Analects** with a stick in the hope that, in an elided referentiality, "they'll get it." There must be something in the pathos of this referential debacle that feeds into the tragic view of the **Cantos'** nobility by virtue of their failed intentions ("a failure of will," in McGann's and many others' estimation), a materialized failure that elicits a psychological complement in the epic authority of Pound. So textual materiality returns very quickly, at least in modernism, to the psychological subject that one would like to exclude from it.

Q: Your essays show an interest in the political instrumentality of language, how politics tries to keep control and retain the power to pursue its own goals. Would redressing the conditions of reading in a very personal way be the ideal manner to reformulate that relationship?

A: I'm not particularly interested in a "very personal" reading as the way to reformulate politics as "impersonal." But my work does contain elusive, often incomprehensible, subjective, libido-driven materials: if not understood in the classical surrealist dialectic of desire, how do they engage the political? Another way to rephrase the question would be, if my work is (hopefully pleasurably) difficult, how does it redress the onslaught of literal, instrumental language that is politics? One way to think about this would be to consider creativity not as a reaction to its context but as a kind of learning, to begin with often "very personal" but at the same time engaging a "social learning." Both as a form of writing and as social engagement my own work is "experimental," in one formulation "the exploration of conceptual meaning and the use of materials whose final form is not entirely resolved." That certainly would describe its conditions of production; each poem begins in a state of "not knowing" itself or what it is going to say, a virtual heap of unprocessed conceptual raw materials. me process of composition draws out recognitions in the materials and possible sequences, orders, and implications; thematic strands stand out in relief much like the "purple snake / Stands out on porcelain tiles" at the opening of **Progress**.

Let us take that purple snake as one moment in which thematic identification is achieved. It so happened that this snake was a graffiti in a very inhospitable pedestrian underpass leading from Lakeshore Drive to Lake Merritt in Oakland. One's being in that passageway is generally accompanied by some kind of apprehension or fear; I bolt for the light at the end of the tunnel right away. The white porcelain as background connotes a kind of hygiene that is anything but the case; the purple spray paint is not genteel. In this scenario, the poem would appear at the outset as a presentation of oppositional but instrumental language, in the way that subway graffiti in New York is said to be subversive by giving evidence of excluded identity. The next such instrumental assertion, however, makes things more difficult: "The idea / *Is* the thing. Skewed by design..." So it is not simply represented content but a presentation tending toward representation, inevitably skewed in its own attempt to do so, that is at issue. Something interior, private, difficult is attempting to achieve explicit, literal, public content and *say something*; so one would perceive the purple snake as coming out of some unknown background (the unsanitary cultural breeding ground of the porcelain tiles) and wanting to make its case.

What is it saying? If we were to take this image as a simple oppositional moment, it would say "the opposite" of, perhaps, the slick, twenty-story apartment building at one end of the tunnel (the building where, for a while, it was rumored Black Panther leader Huey Newton lived). Subway graffiti, likewise, would be the political other to the commuters who confront it each day on their way to work; such a representation would confirm the everyday world "even in its traces" by virtue of a failed opposition. But this representation could also be seen as presenting itself in a different way, as coming out of and perpetuating an irresolution of its own condition; a condition that wants to be redressed, but not in any finality of its own content. The teenagers who painted this design are probably very uneasy about seeing themselves as purple snakes. The instability of this image –which occurs at the same time as its "emergent" social meaning– conveys an intensely private meaning in an agony of public space. It is, at the same time, an act that complicates public space by placing such an unstable, private image within it. The larger world is thereby changed –for the inscriber as much as the viewer; so the snake might be said to have "learned" its way into it. It creates the conditions for the understanding of itself as part of the landscape, as necessary, immediate, and appropriate –but a further context of irresolution obtrudes, and one is faced again with the necessity for further acts. In this case, such further acts will probably be violent. This is not a mild example, and it is not one that typifies my work as a whole. Its position as one of the opening moments of **Progress** is to identify social violence as one of the limiting themes of the poem, as one result of instrumental language. In citing the purple snake, the poem is "thinking with the things as they exist," in Louis Zukofsky's sense; in this way the difficulty of private meanings engages social meanings more generally, in a series of experimental moves. Just as the purple snake is emerging from a blanked and negated background into "saying something" it can scarcely recognize, so private language qualifies the public and creates a new ground on which instrumental meanings can be modified and redefined. It is not simply a matter of opposition.

Q: You say in "The XYZ of Reading" that "the question has become ourselves." Are we able to answer in a pure way, I mean without any contamination of imposed references?

A: The form of a riddle travels through space and time. We
     question a question in order to fill in its form. Its meaning
     is the questioning act. If "existence" is calling itself into
     question, we can easily supply the answer because in that
     case we know; the question has become ourselves.
     (**Conduit**, 12)

Or "hidden is in," as I wrote in **Progress**. As Viktor Shklovsky
has pointed out, a "secret" meaning leads to the defamiliarization
effect: in the juxtaposition of two different interpretations of the
same set of facts –one that we know in the "ordinary" way and
one that we know by virtue of its secret having been revealed– a
"semantic shift" occurs, a frame shift by means of which perception
takes place. An example of this occurs in Marcel Duchamp's
readymade **With Hidden Noise** (1916), which withholds the
"secret" of its depth even from the artist (the readymade is
comprised of a ball of twine bolted between two metal plates on
which some obscure lettering had been pressed; Duchamp had
asked Walter Arensberg to place an object in the hollow of the
twine without telling Duchamp what it was, thus making the
"hidden noise" of the title). Writing of this sculpture as an instance
of the sublime, Jerry Estrin describes it as "a signaling device
whose meaning seems constantly to come from elsewhere, from
a space that has nothing to do with the object." The viewer is left
in the position "only to realize, through a kind of engaged training,
that one can't ever pin down the meaning –meaning always
vanishes and this is its **Noise**." In my own excerpt from "The
XYZ of Reading," substitute "existence" for the Duchampian
readymade; "the question becomes ourselves" by virtue of the
"kind of engaged training" necessary to comprehend it. Meaning
in this sense becomes a kind of practice by virtue of the
interpretative distance necessitated from any of its objects. "Its
meaning is the questioning act."

Calling existence into question, as Duchamp's readymade clearly does (how else could we think of it?), we are left with ourselves; just so, a purely Kantian moment of the sublime would be uncontaminated, like a bolt from the blue. If it is possible to make meaning by virtue of such thought experiments, one would be tempted to answer yes: the question of existence does not involve "imposed references" for its answer. The ratio of two interpretations, one as familiar as Duchamp and one an interpretative secret, seems to produce a moment of "uncontaminated," pure defamiliarization. As a result, it may seem that there are certain effects of "calling existence into question" that can be accomplished with any materials –as long as they are placed in such a relation that their interpretative possibilities are set at odds to reveal them. The arbitrariness is not a pre-given linguistic one, as with Saussure, but a compositional possibility for objects articulated in relation to their contexts. One could therefore "start anywhere" in a series of objective investigations that would call existence into question within specific contexts, leading to a compositional sequence whose meaning would be its "questioning act." This is what I attempt to do with such incremental progressions of disparate propositions, as for example in the poem "Direct Address":

Tripping over a fireplug, think . . . Warren G. Harding wanted to meet Debs.

Abstract from Indo-European.

Thorns that lust and hate.

"In order to make them believe." At the end of history, air molecules on eyes.

Eyes open wide.

The opposite is what I intend.

Parking lots in Fremont convert an image to
X. m is many increments stacked up to be
shipped.

(Conduit, 57)

What Warren G. Harding had to do with Debs (nothing but a
little friendly curiosity for the man the government had been
locking up for some number of years on the part of its chief
executive) is an American non sequitur congruent with, but of
another order than, "parking lots in Fremont." The poem seems
to imply that this relation of dissociation is productive; in fact,
it provides a way that such seemingly incompatible
considerations as the history of the word *abstract* and the
affective qualities of thorns can be reconciled in a temporal
argument. If we imagine that each of such propositions is
"calling existence into questions," we may grant that a
"subjectivity effect" is achieved in the way in which such
progressions "have become ourselves." We are both distanced
from all such assertions and simultaneously producing more
and more of them, as the poem goes on to show. These assertions
continue to "call existence into question," in fact try very hard
to get close:

To go underground and arrive in Berkeley.

And present Adlai Stevenson a degree. The only
trademark is the arbitrary . . .

"That which exists through sunlight is *shade*."

. . . as difficult as meaning itself.

As history discovers the present. . . But impossible
of direct approach!

Coming around a corner, their carts full of goods.
(71)

Here there is not so much a continuous present as a continuous
sublime; in other words, even a proposition that would invoke
the present would be "impossible of direct approach" and thus
double –by that act we interpret it, withholding interpretation.
"Meaning" "itself" is "as difficult." The poem discovers that
the "distance that equals results" here is a social distance; our
meaning-preserving strategies have turned into social
reproduction, whether we like it or not. The production is pure,
uncontaminated –in fact, it could be said prove that only this
world is real, if anyone could call themselves into question
long enough to understand it. They can't; in that sense, the
world as it has proposed itself to us retains the upper hand:
"Increase of cancer in Richmond. In time to build up from the
ground." Reification is not simply imposed on us but is
constructed by specific semantic incongruities that we participate
in, which the experiment in meaning undertaken here sees as
first principles. The references are determined by the entire
method, but they are equally prefigured by the world.

Q: *Progress* is a long epic poem with stanzas of five lines
revisioning history. the world, those immediate facts of

experience, news, and even some characters. What was the conception of that book?

A: I've discussed a number of aspects of the conception(s) behind **Progress** elsewhere, but the topic, like the poem, seems almost inexhaustible. Rather than reading **Progress** in terms of its historical reference to the period in which it was written (the Reagan Recession), one could also read it for its organization of "those immediate facts of experience, news, and even some characters." The notion of "progress" would then veer from that of the former reading, as "difficulty overcome," to other senses equally present: the poem invokes all kinds of "progress," from **Pilgrim's Progress** (millennial horizons), the Progressive Era (standardized tests); the Progressive Labor Party (intellectual violence, breaking chairs over the heads of SDS members); "Work in Progress" (the unfinished project of modernism, Joyce). One that particularly interests me is the notion from Elizabethan times of the "queen's progress," which would describe the course of her state visits accompanied by her retinue through the countryside (for example to Lyme Regis, formerly simply Lyme, hence its new name). If the queen's progress were a form, I imagine representational "nodes" of theatrical display occurring at each designated point in its sequence where the country would be cleaned up and made presentable. This could be read as an amusing comment on the notion of style as a spectacle of social hygiene presented to an absolute observer (citizens of Houston recently undertook such a project in cleaning up all visible trash on the route of the heads of state there for an economic summit). In any case, all such notions of "progress" –along with their static entailments– in the cultural lexicon, would apply.

How then would one describe the construction of meaning in the poem? Alan Liu's recent discussion of "decision trees" in

communication seemed so evocative that I thought I had
embodied them in my writing before I had even read what he
had to say about them. Liu refers to devices of citation out of
which histories are made: "Like 'binaries' in structuralist
decision-trees (left/right, raw/ cooked, bear clan/eagle clan, and
so on), citational devices are the micro-components –the
'switches'– that control narrative signals as they course down
the... decision-trees."[1] Borrowing from Avital Ronnel's **The
Telephone Book**, Liu analogizes the outcomes of these
"decision-trees" to communicative acts that select, by virtue of
the character of their messages, the appropriate receivers (much
like a long-distance phone number –1-800-ABU BAKR, for
example– might select out of all the information in the world
its appropriate destination, in this case the Trinidadian terrorist
Abu Bakr [such is the irony of the world as it is "called up"
by these decision trees; "terrorists" here may be defined as
"what you can call up but can't put back down"]). In any case,
if ideology had been calling us, now we get to call it back:

> We might say that the entire structure of narrative
> communication consists of a network of switchable
> relays allowing citations or "calls" to be put through
> between the narrative subject and its semantically
> significant others: not just the object on the
> predicative trunk line but also the remote authorities
> of the sender, receiver, helper, and opponent on long-
> distance lines. The relation of the latter lines to the
> main narrative trunk, indeed, is precisely that of an
> electronic 'relay' or remote-controlled switching
> mechanism. These relays may be integrated in
> complex patterns to create the circuits that Greimas
> analyses as narrative 'functions' and 'transforma-

tions'; but they all start as devices that from an out-
side location switch the direction of the predicative
line when 'called' upon in an inquiry-loop.

This description of narrative communication (and there are
certainly others, which won't do so well) seems particularly
suited to the nonnarrative progression, the "predicative trunk
line," around which **Progress** is built. In fact, the kind of
overarching narrative that concerns Liu –that of standard literary
histories– could easily be set aside in favor of the constructive
potential of **Progress**'s nonnarrative, "autotelic" form. That is,
one of the calls the trunk line of **Progress** could be processing
through its series of "decision trees" would be its own continuous
meaning –an interpretant continually called upon but never
determinately reached (until the ending –"adding / The date to
a list of days / With astronomical slowness," when at least the
poem is complete). At this point, Liu's conclusion to the
problems he poses is similar to the one I draw from mine: "To
observe the second-order, monitoring technology [the accretive,
cumulative, nonnarrative meaning of **Progress** in my case], we
need now to step off the narrative plane entirely to the real-
world' situation in which [the text, literary history or poem]
functions." Rather than creating an icon of received history,
however, **Progress** intends a demonstration of "new meaning"
that is at the same time both a social and individual "learning"
–a presentation of the world, unlike the theater of the queen's
progress, to be called up on its own authority.
Which returns to the question of the poem's materials, the
micronarratives and citations of "immediate facts of experience,
news, and even some characters" (to which should be added,
of course, "language"). I remember one such "immediate"
moment that became incorporated into the poem in which the

"Mundane Egg" is reflected "in a pool of reflected light.... //
On roof of pool one floor above / Parking lot, / modern living
/ Smashing parked car windows / To make a sound out of
brick" (75-76). I seem in this passage to have shifted from a
"philosophical revery" about hazy mirrors to a remembrance
based on seeing, from the street, the light reflected from an
indoor pool on the ceiling of the fourth story of a modern
apartment building in Oakland, the first three stories of which
were parking lot. This heavenly image contrasted with the
possible fate of cars parked on the street, which might have
their windows broken, thus "calling up" reflections of an
adolescent act of possibly reprehensible behavior: in the eighth
grade, I had gone with a gang of tough boys on an adventure
clearly over my head to the parking lot of a country club near
my house, whereupon they broke a number of car windows. I
didn't and in fact lingered behind at the bottom of the creek
beside it, but we all ran –in fact we were chased by the police–
through the hills. It took over an hour of avoiding the roads
after I had separated from the others (one of whom, Ray, I later
heard ended up in prison –a kind of closure) to get back home.
I was equally innocent and guilty, split down the middle by
remorse either way. Was this remorse appropriate to my present
relation to the elite's pool and its reflected light (earlier in the
poem, "Today's pool is a baroque sky / Not available in
Arkansas")? I then proceed with this self-excoriation to two
narratives in which clearly I was in the wrong –an "eighth
year" escapade in Taiwan that I will not recount in which I was
guilty both as individual delinquent and collective "imperialist,"
but again in two senses, and another moment of excess at age
13 when "I roll[ed a number of large construction] pipes into
a stream / In my wish to speak clearly." The division "called
up" by the reflected light in any case turns out to structure a

"decision-tree" –and such exist at every point in the poem– by which the poem's conceptions are brought into the world: "An entire life to be instructed." The poem is thus truly revisionary, in the sense of overcoming bad history –both my own and others'.

Q: Parentheses play a significant role in "Prison Life" (*1–10*). We may read three different discourses –one of them just the words inserted in the parentheses, another the nonparenthetical words, and finally both together. Is there any specific intention in playing with that device?

A: The device itself came from an early work of Christopher Dewdney's, which as I remember it used parentheses to approximate "word viruses" that would invade and inhabit the host bodies of texts. There was also a question of surface and depth, with the parenthetical words seemingly standing for interpretative depths behind the "text" but at the same time being displaced on its surface (just as right now the word **Colonnades** –the name of a trendy restaurant in early 1980s New York– suddenly surfaces in this account; there weren't any columns beside the name, as I remember it, but the sunken depths of the restaurant, one half flight of stairs down, seemed contained behind them anyway). I was interested in this effect as it would interrupt the textual surface (from the production side, as in Dewdney's poem) and anticipate the resistance of a reader in accepting the authority of the text (on the side of consumption, perhaps , but here as the "interpellation" of alternative meanings, interruptions). If ideology is structured in the way dialogue is subordinated in recorded speech (as for Voloshinov), here the textual surface flips back and forth between the locus of this effect being on the side either of the writer or the reader.

In writing this prose poem, in fact, I was a reader –of a passage from Stan Brakhage's **Film Biographies** that described, in a highly poetic fashion, how the young Sergei Eisenstein must have understood cinematic montage from flipping the pages of the (bourgeois, certainly) stories that would have been read to him. This vaguely preposterous passage seemed also more than true, perhaps by virtue of equally compelling identifications with cinematic montage and the reader-as-boy. If so, these identifications between the public world (cinema as Lenin's most important art) and the private (developmental stages extending back to boyhood and integrated in a continuous "interior speech," in the psychologist Vygotsky's sense) are integrated here in a form of continual interrupting the "exterior" text with all manner of "inner" objections. The moral of such a process for Voloshinov and Vygotsky is clear: inner speech is social. The phenomenal space resulting in the poem –between writer and reader, public and private– aligns with much of what I subsequently wrote; the device is thematically motivated.

Q: Is it desirable to approach a poetry that allows numerous interpretations and that avoids definitive structures with an anti-scientific attitude?

A: As David Antin once said, "Science is the poetry of terror." I see no reason to disagree with that assessment. However, a scientific attitude in exactly that sense is fundamental to aesthetics as we know it. Consider the Renaissance practice of anatomical drawings: then it is not only a particular formal knowledge to be gained from the specific configurations of bones and muscles, but an attitude of distance toward "life studies" to be realized in this knowledge. The example of

Whitman recording his experiences as a hospital nurse in the
Civil War (**Specimen Days**) offers a similar moment in
American literature; Whitman's expansiveness is the predicate
of this inevitable objectification. In poetry of the "late modern"
period –as it was when I entered into it in the late sixties–
however, such exemplary knowledge had been absorbed into a
modernist psychology in which objectification was a form of
"killing off" threats to the unity of the self. The "poetry of
terror" Antin discusses I believe was his way of relocating the
experience of modernist psychology onto a ground of knowledge
that might more "reasonably" be said to occasion it. The move,
of course, made by writers of my own circle was to displace
such psychology onto the objective properties of "language,"
and this seems doubly motivated –in Antin's allegorical sense,
and in an additional one. It would not have been possible in a
time of deep antipathy to the Vietnam War to relocate the
"terror" of modernist psychology onto anything as literal as
objectified knowledge of the body –such a value for science
was not possible in the era of napalm, Agent Orange, and the
draft. The psychology of response to modernist terror that is
found in earlier postmodern work –extending from Olson's
corporeality to the "body art" of Carolee Schneeman– as a
result was to be displaced onto an inchoate, boundless
"language" as a ground of aesthetic distance and source of
positive knowledge. "Language" for us was the fantasy of
objectification that replaced, discontinuously, the physicality of
the earlier postmodernism.
So "a poetry that allows numerous interpretations" as opening
out into "language" would seem to be one solution to the artistic
need for an objectified ground against which the grandeur of life
would stand out. By virtue of its motivation as a form of
postmodernist fantasy, this may lead to a sense of such work as

"avoid[ing] definite structures" –but that ignores the objectification of "language" itself as definite. Such a risk –that "language" is both objective and a form of avoidance– also seems, in this account, to embody frustrating complications, the only excuse for which must be their persistent recurrence as an ethical dilemma. In my view, a poetics of "language" is an attempt to find a workable ground for modernism that leads to real solutions for the dilemmas it proposes. Here again we have "progress" being negotiated in a marvelously conflictual dimension. An "antiscientific" attitude, however, would simply resolve the dilemma in favor of "avoidance," ending only in a kind of regression, a sentimentality not recuperable to its original motives.

Q: In *Plasma/Paralleles/"X"* many lines are just a sentence that we are permitted to think or meditate about: this fact allows for an increase in both information and contrast. Is this a literary device for making us conscious of the continuous superimposition of meanings/speculations that are in conformity with or deform our competence?

A: In all three poems in that book I was conscious of working out of the dilemma you describe –the simultaneous reinforcement and undermining of linguistic competence. In the first poem, "Plasma," this is explicitly thematized:

A paradox is eaten by the space around it.

I'll repeat what I said.

To make a city into a season is to wear sunglasses inside a volcano.

He never forgets his dreams.

The effect of the lack of effect.

me hand tells the eye what to see.

I repress other useless attachments. Chances of
survival are one out of ten.

A paradox, to begin with, would seem to embody opposing
meanings, but even its meaning as a paradox is consumed by
a context that does not recognize any inevitably in such
opposition. This would be the paradigm for the effect of contrast
you mention. Therefore, the repetition that follows is, in exactly
this sense, both paradoxically referring to the previous and
following lines (making them equivalent) and indicating an
autonomous act without **any** preconditions –an announcement
by "I" that he will repeat what he has said. Such a paradox of
repetition (line 2) is being argued to establish a "meta"
continuity, but at the outset it is unclear whether the "paradox"
of line 1 is the "same as" the difficult analogy of line 3 –whether
the interpretative dilemmas already proposed could be understood
as a mapping of the cognitive onto the performative ("To make
a city into a season is to wear sunglasses inside a volcano").
The point that should be increasingly clear as the work is both
performed and interpreted is that there is a substrate in which
"language" itself speaks, not just is spoken by a speaker. This
devolution of phenomena to noumena is the meditation of the
poem, so that "Such is night in the mountains" should be read,
at the end, as a both familiar and unearthly "suchness." And so
it goes: the generation of paradoxical interpretations that cancel
themselves out is the determination of "language" in the work.

Later, in "X," such a continuous self-canceling is meditated on, additionally, in terms of an architectonic of surfaces and origins that is given specific cultural coordinates, in this poem the cultural topography of Los Angeles seen through the incommensurate fact that I happened to have been born there. The competence lost is that which would try to understand a meaning other than the present surface; the competence gained is that which would be oriented toward noumena: "A fact is what you can't get past," and the name for that fact is "language."

Q: I've not found any characters in *Opera—Works*. Are the words the real characters of this world?

A: **Opera—Works** was trying, first of all, to work out of the confines of "persona" that were the dominant poetics of the period (early 1970s). The goal for such poetry was "to find your own voice," the achievement of modestly idiosyncratic style being the guarantee of negotiability in the existing (largely academic) marketplace for otherwise indistinguishable work; the great American conundrum of normativity and individuality, "the one and the many," was being argued out again and again. Against that, I identified with two opposing possibilities: one, a writing that would theatrically display itself without need for persona (here the prior example was Zukofsky); two, a writing that would find a natural order in syntax by enacting its own processes (here the prior example was romantic prose, from De Quincey and Coleridge to Ginsberg and Creeley). Roughly, these two poles demonstrate the split between "Opera" (theatrical display) and "Works" (writing) the title.
While "persona" is being critically modified in this work, I don't think anything like "words [as] characters" was the outcome. There are, in fact, "characters" who function as words

in a number of the poems, the first of which is an "ode" to "Bourbaki," a mythological figure invented as the author of the work of a circle of French mathematicians (the "Bourbaki circle") in the 1920s. As an identity Bourbaki is a construction, an intentional agent built in much the same way that the proofs or lemmas ascribed to him were made. Bourbaki himself appears in the poem only as his name; he is very like the character in "I saw a man climb up on the roof behind them, do Yoga all day" or "Man laughs randomly" or Wittgenstein in "Dream: With Wittgenstein." Later I essay the entire construction of such exteriorized identity in "Export Diplomat": "There are plenty of references to Mayakovsky on the Nevsky Prospect, not needing any statues." Identity devolves into language, in the process, a dilemma I willfully proposed. Or such is what I would now like to think: now, I read a stanza like "The troops are departing by boat / I can see them / but think of myself— / as better than nature" and realize how little aware I could have been at the time of the outer horizons of identification I would need to negotiate once the poetry of persona had been abandoned.

Q: You have been widely regarded as an innovative and dynamic leader among the "language" poets during the 1980s. How do you see the debate about Poetics that took place during those years?

A: It is accurate to say that the debates in the 1980s were more about poetics than poetry; in the 1970s the emphasis was on poetic forms apart from poetics, while in the early 1980s the shift was toward theory, with poetic practice often standing as a place holder. In many theoretical articles about the work of the language school from that period, bite-sized chunks of "language writing" were often served up as more-or-less arbitrary, exchangeable examples. The same argumentative strategy would not apply today: the explanatory moment of "language writing" in general is no longer so important, while debates in poetics now seem tied more to specific (if theorized) extensions of poetic practice. Such a fruitful synthesis of theory and practice has been under way since the mid 1980s.

Briefly, **This**, which I edited from 1971, printed only verse and prose; one of the central issues in the publication was formal: What are the differences between lyric poetry and poetic prose? **L=A=N=G=U=A=G=E** (1978-82), as is well known, printed primarily brief statements by writers and artists that established a theoretical ground for already existing practice. The form of **L=A=N=G=U=A=G=E** was important, with the equal signs of the title standing for a field of related work, a kind of poetic matrix. In its imitation of equivalence, and in the subjective relativity of particular practices, this form led to questions later in the decade about the recuperation of "language writing" to romanticism. **Poetics Journal**, which I have co-edited since 1981, publishes longer, more thematic articles while at the same time occasionally publishing creative work that stands in the place of theory. One thing we did, starting with the second issue, was to introduce "theme" titles such as "Close Reading," "Poetry and Philosophy," "Women and Language," "Non/ Narrative," and so on. While it is true that much of the work we published could have been categorized under any or all of these titles, the loose thematic organization each suggested worked to draw out more particular inferences. A dialogue between, rather than an equivalence of, theory and practice has been our editorial goal. By extension, this dialogue would lead to various kinds of postmodern cultural engagement.

In retrospect, then, I see the debate about poetics that took place in early 1980s, from the conclusion of **L=A=N=G=U-A-G=E** to the beginning of **Poetics Journal**, to have shifted from concerns of theoretical equivalence to ones of formal argument. The overlap is great, but still I think the somewhat mystificatory presentation of "language writing" that, say, Charles Bernstein made in "The Conspiracy of Us" (to be further toyed with in his maxim "Schools are made to be broken") would no longer apply, and that more specific interactions –for example, the exchange that has been developing between American and Soviet writers in the last few issues of **Poetics Journal**– are the wave of the future. In this sense, a shift in the direction from synchronic equivalence to diachronic argument has been, tentatively, one outcome of these debates.

Q: You have taken a big step in trying to liberate language from any form of power. How do you evaluate the possibilities of that proposal in the 1990s as opposed to in the 1960s?

A: I cannot say, in May 1991 as I write this, that "for us the primary reality is the war," as Sartre did in 1944. The primary reality for a brief and spasmodic time frame in January-February 1991 *was* the Gulf War, and we can cite this as an explicit replay of an earlier period, 1964-75, in which the primary *unreality* was the Vietnam War. We now live, and are writing within, a social order that has paradoxically become fully mobilized for "permanent war" and yet purports to suspend all hostilities in a Pax Americana. This instrumental socious is articulated to a high degree, and surely "language" has been a primary means of its reproduction. The writer in this environment is going to have particular tasks; it is no accident that, recently, the *only* sector of society that was identifiably

against the Gulf War was that configured around the arts. The
role of the writer at present is to maintain a fundamental
perspective in social and cultural reality that would not exist
–that would be destroyed without his or her efforts.

[1] Alan Liu, "Flat Literary History: Literariness and Postmodern General Literature," part 1,
"The Bug in the Book: Toward a Critique of Technology," Paper presented at a conference
on "What Is Literary History?," University of California, Berkeley, March 1991.

ACT-9576   3/4/95

PS
325
B75
1992

El Productor S. L. - Depósito Legal TF 1747/92